Renal Diet Cookbook for Beginners

A step-by-step cookbook for newly diagnosed patients with all the nutrition facts they need to know.

AILEEN WILLIAMSON

© Copyright 2021 AILEEN WILLIAMSON All rights reserved.

This document is geared towards providing exact and reliable information in regard to the topic and issue covered. The publication is sold with the idea that the publisher is not required to render accounting, officially permitted, or otherwise, qualified services. If advice is necessary, legal, or professional, a practiced individual in the profession should be ordered.

- From a Declaration of Principles which was accepted and approved equally by a Committee of the American Bar Association and a Committee of Publishers and Associations.

In no way is it legal to reproduce, duplicate, or transmit any part of this document in either electronic means or in printed format. Recording of this publication is strictly prohibited, and any storage of this document is not allowed unless with written permission from the publisher. All rights reserved.

The information provided herein is stated to be truthful and consistent, in that any liability, in terms of inattention or otherwise, by any usage or abuse of any policies, processes, or directions contained within is the solitary and utter responsibility of the recipient reader. Under no circumstances will any legal responsibility or blame be held against the publisher for any reparation, damages, or monetary loss due to the information herein, either directly or indirectly.

Respective authors own all copyrights not held by the publisher.

The information herein is offered for informational purposes solely and is universal as so. The presentation of the information is without contract or any type of guarantee assurance.

The trademarks that are used are without any consent, and the publication of the trademark is without permission or backing by the trademark owner. All trademarks and brands within this book are for clarifying purposes only and are owned by the owners themselves, not affiliated with this document.

Table of Contents

Introduction 8

Chapter 1: Breakfast 10

   Turkey Breakfast Burritos 10

   Loaded Veggie Eggs 12

   Bagel 14

   Microwave Egg White French Toast 15

   Scrambled Eggs 16

   Chocolate Pancakes With Moon Pie Filling 18

   Breakfast Biscuits 20

   Egg Cups 22

   Egg and Sausage Sandwich 24

   Blueberry Muffs 25

   Fluffy Buttermilk Pancake 27

   Sausage Pattie 29

   Beach Omelet 31

   French Toast Custar 33

Chapter 2: Lunch 35

   Egg Fried Rice 35

   Zucchini Turkey Burger 37

   Veggie Vindaloo with Naan 38

   BBQ Chicken Pita Pizza 41

   Cheesy Beef Burger 42

   Savory Chicken Wraps 44

   Shrimp Quesadill 45

   Yummy Tacos with Mexican Seasoning 47

   Tortilla Beef Swirls 49

   Chicken and Gnocchi Dumplings 51

   Chicken Fajita Strips 53

   Chicken Brunswick Broth 54

   Fried Green Tomatoes 57

 Savory Meat Loa 59

Chapter 3: Dinner **62**
 Chicken Pie Stew 62

 Tasty Green Beans 64

 Lemon Chicken 66

 Sautéed Greens and Pork Chops 68

 Stir Fried Collard Greens 71

 Zesty Tilapia 73

 Spicy Beef Stir-Fry 75

 Herbed Rice 77

 Roasted Lamb Leg 78

 Skirt Steak With Bourbon Glaze 80

 Roast Loin Pork With Apple Stuffing 82

 Rice & Cauliflower Cakes 85

 Pork Cutlets and Sautéed Vegetable 87

 Crispy Brussels Sprouts 89

Chapter 4: Desserts **91**
 Crispy Cups with Fresh Berries 91

 Lemon Squares 93

 Pumpkin Strudel 95

 Orange and Cinnamon Biscotti 97

 Rustic Apple Cinnamon Filled Phyllo Pastries 100

 Delicious Berry Bread Pudding 103

 Ginger And Lemon Coconut Cookies 105

 Mouth Watering Cranberry Fruit Bars 107

 Minty Chocolate Brownies 109

 Sugar And Cream Cheese Cookies 110

 Lemon Cupcakes 112

 Blueberry and Apple Crisp 114

Chapter 5: Beverages **116**
 Lemonade 116

 Apple Cinnamon Cider 118

Chocolate Smoothie 119

Blueberry Smoothie 121

Masala Chai Tea 122

Apple And Beet Juice 124

Fabulous Hot Cocoa 125

Chocolate Shake 126

Pineapple Protein Smoothie 128

Fruity Smoothie 129

Snow Cone Smoothie 130

Cinnamon and Hazelnut Coffee 131

Spiced Eggnog 132

Chapter 6: Soups 134

Sweet Cherry Soup 134

Chicken Noodle Soup 136

Gnocchi and Chicken Dumplings 138

Carrot and Cabbage Soup 139

Vegetable Soup 141

Minestrone Soup 144

Apple Soup and Smoked Chicken 146

Chicken Noodle Soup 148

Tuscan Vegetable Soup 150

Carrot and Ginger Soup 152

Parsnip and Pear Soup 154

Red Lentil Soup 156

Kidney Bean and Vegetable Soup 158

Navy Bean Stew 160

Barley & Vegetable Soup 162

Chapter 7: Snacks 165

Egg Muffs 165

Turkey In Buns 167

Maple And Honey Trail Mix 169

Heavenly Challah 171

Spicy Turkey Barbecue Wings 173

Cinnamon and Orange Biscotti 175

Buffalo Chicken Salad Stuffed In Cucumber Cups 177

Herbed Biscuits 179

Yummy Protein Bars 181

Almond Pecan Caramel Corn 182

Quiche 184

Mix Snacks 186

Chapter 8: Salads 188

Goat Cheese and Strawberry Spring Salad 188

Summer Salad 190

Cucumber Salad 191

Kidney Bean Salad With Dijon Vinaigrette 192

Apple and Chicken Salad 194

Chicken and Lemon Curry Salad 196

Colorful Garden Salad 197

Chicken Fruit Salad 199

Grilled Chicken Salad 200

Pineapple Coleslaw 202

Italian Eggplant Salad 204

Crunchy Chicken Salad 205

Cool Coconut Marshmallow Salad 207

Italian Chicken Salad 208

Purple Salad 210

Chapter 9: Pasta 212

Cheesy Pasta with Meat Sauce 212

Pasta Primavera 214

Pesto Pronto 216

Vegetable Pasta Salad 217

Creamy Lemon Salmon Pasta 220

Pasta With Kidney Bean Sauce 222

Cheese and Macaroni 224

Baked Broccoli and Cauliflower Mac-n-Cheese 225

Creamy Shells With Bacon and Peas 228

Ranch Chicken Pasta 230

Creamy Sweet Potato Pasta Bake 232

Chicken Enchilada Pasta 234

Simple Beef Ragu 237

Spicy Pasta with Chicken 239

Skillet Chicken Pasta with Crispy Sage 242

Chapter 10: Sea food **245**

Broccoli Fettuccine and Creamy Shrimp 245

Fish Tacos 247

Zesty Orange Tilapia 249

Classic Spicy Shrimp and Linguine 251

Creamy Shrimp and Broccoli Fettuccine 253

Shrimp Fried Rice 255

Super Tuesday Shrimp 257

Shrimp-Stuffed Deviled Eggs 259

Honey Glazed Salmon 260

Foil Baked Pimento Cod Fillet 262

Mediterranean Baked Trout 264

Shrimp Scampi 266

Oven Fried Fish 268

Shrimp and Cabbage Stir-Fry 270

Seared Tuna Steak 272

Spicy fish stew 273

Steamed Fish and Vegetables 275

Conclusion **278**

Introduction

What is a renal diet?

A renal diet is a low-sodium, low-phosphorous, and low-protein diet. A renal diet stresses the value of eating high-quality protein and, in most cases, reducing fluid intake. Some patients may also require potassium and calcium restrictions. Since every person's body is different, it's vital that each individual works with a renal dietitian to establish a diet that's customized to their unique needs.

Sodium:

Sodium is a mineral that can be found in almost all-natural foods. The words "salt" and "sodium" are also used interchangeably. Salt, on the other hand, is a sodium-chloride compound. Salt or sodium in other types can be present in the foods we consume. Because of the added salt, processed foods also have higher sodium levels.

For people with kidney disease, too much sodium may be dangerous because their kidneys are unable to properly remove excess fluid and sodium from the body.

For people with kidney disease, too much sodium may be dangerous because their kidneys are unable to effectively remove unwanted fluid and sodium from the body. When the tissues and bloodstream accumulate sodium and fluid, it causes high blood pressure, swelling in the face, hands, and legs, increased thirst, shortness of breath, and heart failure.

Potassium:

Potassium is a mineral that can be present in a variety of foods as well as in the human body. Potassium helps to maintain a steady heartbeat and keeps the muscles in good working order. Potassium is also needed to keep the bloodstream's electrolyte and fluid balance. The kidneys aid in maintaining a healthy potassium balance in the body by excreting excess potassium into the urine.

As the kidneys malfunction, the body's potassium levels rise because the kidneys are unable to remove excess potassium. Hyperkalemia is a condition in which there is too much potassium in the blood. It causes slow pulse, heart attacks, muscle weakness, an irregular heartbeat, and death.

Phosphorus:

Phosphorus is an important mineral for bone health and growth. Phosphorus is also essential for the growth of connective tissue and organs, as well as the movement of muscles. When phosphorus-rich food is eaten and digested, the phosphorus is absorbed by the small intestines and retained in the bones.

Additional phosphorus in your blood can be removed by normal functioning kidneys. If kidney function is impaired, the kidneys are unable to remove excess phosphorus from the body. High phosphorus levels will deplete the calcium in your bones, causing them to become brittle. Calcium deposits that occur in the blood vessels, eyes, lungs, and heart are also a risk.

Protein

Protein is not a concern for kidneys that are in good condition. Protein is normally absorbed, and waste products are generated, which are then filtered by the kidney's nephrons. The waste is then transferred to urine with the aid of additional renal proteins. Damaged kidneys, on the other hand, struggle to eliminate protein waste, which then builds up in the blood.

Hence, this book is a treasure chest of recipes for people who want to start a renal diet without removing their favorite foods.

Chapter 1: Breakfast

Turkey Breakfast Burritos

Total Time: 30 minutes

Servings: 8

Difficulty level: low

Ingredients:

- One-Fourth cup fresh yellow, green, or red diced bell peppers
- One pound of ground turkey
- One-Fourth cup canola oil
- Eight-to-six-inch flour burrito shells
- One-Fourth cup diced onions
- Eight beaten eggs, scrambled
- Two tablespoons freshly chopped scallions
- Two tablespoons seeded jalapeño peppers
- Two tablespoons freshly chopped cilantro

- Half teaspoon smoked paprika
- One-Fourth teaspoon chili powder
- One cup shredded cheddar cheese

Directions:

Step 1

In half of the oil, sauté the onions, meatloaf, scallions, peppers and cilantro until translucent. Stir in the spices, and then take it off the heat.

Step 2

In a separate large sauté pan, heat the scrambled eggs and remaining oil over medium-high heat.

Step 3

Fill the burrito shells with equal quantities of meatloaf mix, vegetables, eggs, and cheese, then fold and serve.

Nutrition Facts:

Per Serving:
- ✓ Calories 407 cal
- ✓ Sodium 513 mg
- ✓ Protein 25 g
- ✓ Cholesterol 237 mg
- ✓ Fat 24 g
- ✓ Potassium 285 mg
- ✓ Carbohydrates 23 g
- ✓ Fiber 2 g
- ✓ Phosphorus 359 mg

> ✓ Calcium 209 mg

Loaded Veggie Eggs

Total Time: 15 minutes

Servings: 2

Difficulty level: low

Ingredients:

- One-Fourth cup chopped bell pepper
- One-Fourth cup onion, chopped
- Three cups of fresh spinach
- One minced garlic clove
- Four whole eggs
- One-Fourth teaspoon black pepper
- One cup cauliflower
- One tablespoon oil of choice
- Fresh spring onion and parsley for garnish

Directions:

Step 1

Set aside eggs that have been whisked with pepper until light and fluffy.

Step 2

In a large skillet, heat the oil over medium heat.

Step 3

In a pan, sauté the peppers and onions until the peppers are aromatic and golden.

Step 4

Add the garlic and whisk quickly to mix before adding the spinach and cauliflower.

Step 5

Vegetables are sautéed, then reduced to medium-low heat and covered for five minutes.

Step 6

Add the eggs to the vegetables and mix with a whisk.

Step 7

Top with spring onions or fresh parsley until the eggs are completely cooked.

Nutrition Facts:

Per Serving:
- ✓ Calories 240
- ✓ Sodium 195 mg
- ✓ Protein 15.3 g
- ✓ Cholesterol 372 mg
- ✓ Fat 16.6 g
- ✓ Potassium 605.2 mg
- ✓ Carbohydrate 7.8 g
- ✓ Fiber 2.7 g
- ✓ Phosphorus 253.6 mg
- ✓ Calcium 63 mg

Bagel

Total Time: 5 minutes

Servings: 2

Difficulty level: low

Ingredients:

- One teaspoon low-sodium lemon pepper seasoning
- Two tablespoons cream cheese
- Two red onion slices
- One 2 oz. bagel
- Two ¼ inch thick tomato slices

Directions:

Step 1

Toast a bagel by slicing it in half and toasting it on both sides until nicely browned.

Step 2

Scatter cream cheese on both halves of the bagel. Sprinkle with lemon pepper and finish with onion and tomato slices.

Nutrition Facts:

Per Serving:
- ✓ Calories 134
- ✓ Sodium 219 mg
- ✓ Protein 5 g
- ✓ Cholesterol 15 mg
- ✓ Fat 6 g
- ✓ Potassium 162 mg

- ✓ Carbohydrates 19 g
- ✓ Fiber 1.6 g
- ✓ Phosphorus 50 mg
- ✓ Calcium 9 mg

Microwave Egg White French Toast

Total Time: 5 minutes

Servings: 1

Difficulty level: low

Ingredients:

- Two tablespoons sugar-free syrup
- One slice of bread
- Half cup egg whites
- One teaspoon unsalted butter, softened

Directions:

Step 1

Butter the bread and place it on a cutting board. Cut it into small cubes.

Step 2

Place buttered bread cubes into a microwave-safe cup.

Step 3

Cover the bread with the egg whites.

Step 4

Drizzle with the syrup.

Step 5

Microwave for one minute, then push up the sides of the egg white to allow the uncooked egg to spill out around the edges.

Step 6

Continue to microwave for another minute or until the egg is set.

Nutrition Facts:

Per Serving:
- ✓ Calories 200
- ✓ Sodium 415 mg
- ✓ Protein 15 g
- ✓ Cholesterol 11 mg
- ✓ Fat 5 g
- ✓ Potassium 235 mg
- ✓ Carbohydrates 24 g
- ✓ Fiber 0.7 g
- ✓ Phosphorus 54 mg
- ✓ Calcium 50 mg

Scrambled Eggs

Total Time: 15 minutes

Servings: 1

Difficulty level: low

Ingredients:

- One tablespoon crumbled goat cheese

- Two large eggs
- One teaspoon dried dill weed
- One-Eighth teaspoon black pepper

Directions:

Step 1

In a mixing bowl, whisk together the eggs, then pour into a fry pan set over medium heat.

Step 2

Season the eggs with dill weed and black pepper.

Step 3

Continue to cook until the eggs are scrambled.

Step 4

Before eating, sprinkle with crumbled goat cheese.

Nutrition Facts:

Per Serving:
- ✓ Calories 194
- ✓ Sodium 213 mg
- ✓ Protein 16 g
- ✓ Cholesterol 434 mg
- ✓ Calcium 214 mg
- ✓ Fat 14 g
- ✓ Potassium 192 mg
- ✓ Carbohydrates 1 g

- ✓ Fiber 0.2 g
- ✓ Phosphorus 250 mg

Chocolate Pancakes With Moon Pie Filling

Total Time: 20 minutes

Servings: 12

Difficulty level: low

Ingredients:

Moon Pie:

- Half cup marshmallow cream
- One-Fourth cup heavy cream
- One tablespoon unsweetened cocoa powder
- Half cup softened cream cheese

Chocolate Pancakes:

- One cup 2% milk
- Two-Third cup vanilla whey protein powder
- One cup of flour
- Three tablespoons unsweetened cocoa powder
- Three tablespoons sugar
- Half teaspoon baking soda
- One egg
- Two tablespoons canola oil
- One tablespoon lemon juice

- Two teaspoons vanilla extract

Directions:

Moon Pie Filling:

Step 1

When beating the cocoa and heavy cream together, they will eventually start to form stiff peaks. Stop beating at this point.

Step 2

Add cheese, marshmallow cream, and if possible use a protein powder for added texture. Beat for around two more minutes, but do not beat vigorously. Once done, let it rest in the refrigerator.

Pancakes:

Step 1

In a big mixing bowl, combine all the dry ingredients and set aside.

Step 2

In a medium-size mixing bowl, combine all the wet ingredients.

Step 3

Gently fold the wet ingredients into dry ingredients until they are combined, but do not over-mix.

Step 4

Cook the pancakes over medium heat, or 375° F, on a lightly oiled griddle.

Step 5

Using approximately 1/8 cup of batter, shape 4-inch pancakes and flip when they begin to bubble.

Step 6

Distribute equal amounts of Moon Pie Filling to the first twelve pancakes; top with the remaining twelve pancakes and serve dusted with icing sugar.

Nutrition Facts:

> *Per Serving:*
> - ✓ Calories 195
> - ✓ Sodium 121 mg
> - ✓ Protein 7 g
> - ✓ Cholesterol 36 mg
> - ✓ Fat 9 g
> - ✓ Potassium 135 mg
> - ✓ Carbohydrates 22 g
> - ✓ Fiber 1 g
> - ✓ Phosphorus 134 mg
> - ✓ Calcium 67 mg

Breakfast Biscuits

Total Time: 20 minutes

Servings: 12

Difficulty level: low

Ingredients:

- Three-Fourth cup milk
- Two cups flour
- Half teaspoon baking soda
- One tablespoon lemon juice
- One tablespoon honey or sugar
- Eight tablespoons softened unsalted butter

<u>Filling:</u>

- Four eggs
- One cup shredded cheddar cheese
- Eight oz reduced-sodium bacon (chopped)
- One-Fourth cup thinly sliced scallions

Directions:

Step 1

Preheat oven to 425° F.

<u>Filling:</u>

Step 2

Slightly undercook the scrambled eggs.

Step 3

Cook the bacon in a skillet until crispy.

Step 4

Combine all four ingredients in a mixing bowl and set aside.

<u>Dough:</u>

Step 5

In a big mixing bowl, whisk together all dry ingredients.

Step 6

Using a fork or pastry cutter, cut the unsalted butter until it's pea-sized.

Step 7

Make a well in the middle of the mixture, and add the milk and lemon juice.

Step 8

Line, or gently grease and flour, the sides and the bottom of the muffin tins.

Step 9

Scoop fourteen cups of batter into the muffin tins.

Step 10

Bake for twelve minutes or until golden brown at 425° F.

Nutrition Facts:

> *Per Serving:*
> - Calories 330
> - Sodium 329 mg
> - Protein 11 g
> - Cholesterol 105 mg
> - Fat 23 g
> - Potassium 152 mg
> - Carbohydrates 19 g
> - Fiber 1 g
> - Phosphorus 170 mg
> - Calcium 107 mg

Egg Cups

Total Time: 15 minutes

Servings: 12

Difficulty level: low

Ingredients:

- Three cups cooked rice
- Four oz. diced green chilies
- Four oz. shredded cheddar cheese

- Half teaspoon black pepper
- Two oz. diced pimentos
- Two beaten eggs
- Half cup skim milk
- Half teaspoon ground cumin
- Nonstick cooking spray

Directions:

Step 1

Combine 2 oz. cheese, rice, chilies, milk, pimentos, eggs, pepper, and cumin in a big bowl.

Step 2

Using a nonstick cooking spray, coat muffin cups.

Step 3

Distribute the mixture equally between 12 muffin cups. Sprinkle the remaining 2 oz. of shredded cheese on top of each cup.

Step 4

Bake for fifteen minutes at 400° F or until set.

Nutrition Facts:

Per Serving:
- ✓ Calories 109
- ✓ Sodium 79 mg
- ✓ Protein 5 g
- ✓ Cholesterol 41 mg
- ✓ Fat 4 g

- ✓ Potassium 82 mg
- ✓ Carbohydrates 13 g
- ✓ Fiber 0.5 g
- ✓ Phosphorus 91 mg
- ✓ Calcium 91 mg

Egg and Sausage Sandwich

Total Time: 2 minutes

Servings: 1

Difficulty level: low

Ingredients:

- One turkey sausage patty
- One-Fourth cup liquid low-cholesterol egg substitute
- One English muffin
- One tablespoon shredded natural sharp cheddar cheese
- Nonstick cooking spray

Directions:

Step 1

Pour the egg product into a medium skillet coated with non-stick cooking spray and prepare over medium heat. When the egg appears to be almost done, flip it over with a spoon and cook for an additional thirty seconds.

Step 2

Toast the English muffin.

Step 3

Arrange the turkey sausage patty on a tray, cover with a paper towel, and microwave for 1 minute or until cooked according to package directions.

Step 4

Arrange scrambled eggs on an English muffin. Put sausage patty on top, followed by cheddar cheese and the remaining muffin half.

Nutrition Facts:

Per Serving:
- ✓ Calories 253
- ✓ Sodium 591 mg
- ✓ Protein 17 g
- ✓ Cholesterol 32 mg
- ✓ Fat 9 g
- ✓ Potassium 218 mg
- ✓ Carbohydrates 26 g
- ✓ Fiber 2.0 g
- ✓ Phosphorus 158 mg
- ✓ Calcium 174 mg

Blueberry Muffs

Total Time: 1 hour

Servings: 12

Difficulty level: low

Ingredients:

- Two and a half cups fresh blueberries

- One and a half cups sugar
- Half cup unsalted butter
- Two cups 1% milk
- Two eggs
- Two teaspoons baking powder
- Two cups all-purpose flour
- Half teaspoon salt

Directions:

Step 1

Using a low speed mixer, cream together sugar and margarine until smooth and fluffy.

Step 2

Add the eggs one at a time, mixing well after each addition.

Step 3

Sift dry ingredients into a large mixing bowl and combine alternately with milk.

Step 4

Using a fork, mash half a cup blueberries and fold in by hand. Then, by hand, stir in the remaining blueberries.

Step 5

Coat the pan and muffin tins with vegetable oil, then arrange the muffin cups in them.

Step 6

Fill each muffin cup almost to the brim with muffin mixture and sprinkle sugar on the top of each.

Step 7

Bake for 25 to 30 minutes at 375° F. Allow at least 30 minutes for cooling in the pan before carefully removing.

Nutrition Facts:

Per Serving:
- ✓ Calories 275
- ✓ Cholesterol 53 mg
- ✓ Fat 9 g
- ✓ Sodium 210 mg
- ✓ Protein 5 g
- ✓ Carbohydrates 44 g
- ✓ Phosphorus 100 mg
- ✓ Fiber 1.3 g
- ✓ Potassium 121 mg
- ✓ Calcium 108 mg

Fluffy Buttermilk Pancake

Total Time: 15 minutes

Servings: 9

Difficulty level: low

Ingredients:

- One teaspoon cream of tartar
- Two cups all-purpose flour
- Half cup canola oil
- One and a half teaspoons baking soda

- Two cups low-fat buttermilk
- Two tablespoons sugar
- Two large eggs

Directions:

Step 1

Preheat a skillet over a medium heat.

Step 2

In a big mixing bowl, combine the dry ingredients, then add them to the buttermilk, oil, and egg mixture. Mix the dry ingredients with a whisk or spoon until fully moist.

Step 3

Grease the skillet with a tablespoon of canola oil. Scoop the pancake batter into the skillet using a 13-cup measuring cup. Each pancake can spread to approximately 4 inches in diameter. Allow approximately 2 inches between the pancakes to facilitate flipping. Use a spatula to flip pancakes, do so when the bubbles on the base of the pancakes have largely vanished. Allow the opposite side to brown until the middle appears to be dry.

Step 4

Transfer to a serving bowl.

Step 5

Serve with organic berries and eggs for a healthy twist.

Nutrition Facts:

Per Serving:
- ✓ Calories 217
- ✓ Cholesterol 44 mg

- ✓ Fat 9 g
- ✓ Carbohydrates 27 g
- ✓ Phosphorus 100 mg
- ✓ Fiber 1 g
- ✓ Sodium 330 mg
- ✓ Protein 6 g
- ✓ Potassium 182 mg
- ✓ Calcium 74 mg

Sausage Pattie

Total Time: 35 minutes

Servings: 16

Difficulty level: low

Ingredients:

- Two lbs. ground lean pork
- Half cup onion, finely chopped
- Two teaspoons dried sage
- Two tablespoons olive oil
- One teaspoon finely chopped fresh thyme
- One teaspoon fresh ground black pepper
- A pinch of crushed red pepper flakes
- One tablespoon sugar or brown sugar
- A pinch of ground cloves
- One large egg yolk

Directions:

Step 1

Cook the onion in olive oil over a moderately low heat, stirring periodically, for 8 to10 minutes, or until onions are brown.

Step 2

Allow 10 minutes to cool.

Step 3

Mix the sage, red and black pepper, sugar, thyme and cloves in a small bowl.

Step 4

In a big mixing bowl, combine the pork, egg yolk, and reserved onion, then add the mixed spices.

Step 5

Combine thoroughly.

Step 6

Divide the mixture into 16 patties, each weighing 2 ounces.

Step 7

In a large frying pan over medium high heat, cook the patties for 5 minutes on each side or until an internal temperature of 160 degrees is reached.

Nutrition Facts:

Per Serving:
- ✓ Calories: 173.3
- ✓ Fat 14 g
- ✓ Cholesterol 53.9 mg
- ✓ Carbohydrate 1.5 g

- ✓ Sodium 32.5 mg
- ✓ Protein 9.8 g
- ✓ Fiber 0.1 g
- ✓ Calcium 40 mg
- ✓ Phosphorus 120 mg
- ✓ Potassium 300 mg

Beach Omelet

Total Time: 10 minutes

Servings: 1

Difficulty Level: low

Ingredients:

- Two tablespoons chopped onion
- One teaspoon canola oil
- Two tablespoons shredded and frozen hash browns
- Two egg whites
- Two tablespoons soy milk
- Two tablespoons diced fresh green bell pepper
- Two whole eggs
- Two sprigs fresh parsley

Directions:

Step 1

In a frying pan, heat the oil. Add the diced onion and green pepper, and sauté for two minutes.

Step 2

Cook hash browns for five minutes.

Step 3

Combine eggs and soy milk in a mixing bowl.

Step 4

In a separate non-stick skillet, pour egg mixture and cook over medium heat until the omelet firms up.

Step 5

Spoon the hash brown mixture into the center of the omelet surface and use a spatula to loosen both sides of the omelet before rolling it over onto a serving plate.

Step 6

Season with parsley sprigs and additional spices as desired.

Nutrition Facts:

Per Serving:
- Calories 228
- Carbohydrates 12 g
- Protein 15 g
- Fat 13 g
- Sodium 180 mg
- Cholesterol 165 mg
- Potassium 307 mg
- Calcium 38 mg
- Phosphorus 128 mg
- Fiber 0.9 g

French Toast Custar

Total Time: 50 minutes

Servings: 4

Difficulty Level: low

Ingredients:

- Half cup sugar
- One teaspoon cinnamon
- Four cups non-enriched rice milk
- Four tablespoons unsalted melted margarine
- One teaspoon almond extract
- Four slices Italian bread
- Two cups liquid egg substitute (low cholesterol)
- Powdered sugar

Directions:

Step 1

Coat the base and sides of a 9" x 13" baking pan with margarine or non-stick cooking spray.

Step 2

Cover the bottom part of the pan with a layer of bread slices.

Step 3

Combine egg substitute, non-enriched rice milk, sugar, almond extract, melted margarine, and cinnamon in a mixing bowl. Spill over slices of bread.

Step 4

Refrigerate plate, wrapped in plastic wrap, overnight.

Step 5

Preheat oven to 350° F.

Step 6

Bake for 40–50 mins, or until a knife inserted in the middle comes out clean. Dust with confectioners sugar, if required. Serve immediately.

Nutrition Facts:

Per Serving:
- Calories 450
- Carbohydrates 65 g
- Protein 16 g
- Cholesterol 0 mg
- Calcium 86 mg
- Fat 14 g
- Sodium 390 mg
- Phosphorus 111 mg
- Potassium 221 mg
- Fiber .8 g

Chapter 2: Lunch

Egg Fried Rice

Total Time: 10 minutes

Servings: 10

Difficulty level: low

Ingredients:

- Two teaspoons dark sesame oil
- Two eggs
- Two egg whites
- One tablespoon canola oil
- One cup bean sprouts
- One-Third cup green onions, chopped
- Four cups cooked rice, cold
- One cup frozen peas, thawed
- One-Fourth teaspoon ground black pepper

Directions:

Step 1

In a small cup, whisk together the eggs, sesame oil, and egg whites. Combine thoroughly and set aside.

Step 2

In a non-stick skillet, heat canola oil over medium-high heat.

Step 3

Add the egg mixture and cook, stirring constantly, until finished.

Step 4

Sprinkle green onions and bean sprouts on top. Fry for two minutes.

Step 5

Stir in peas and rice. Stir-fry until fully heated.

Step 6

Sprinkle with freshly ground black pepper and serve warm.

Nutrition Facts:

Per Serving:
- ✓ Calories 137
- ✓ Cholesterol 37 mg
- ✓ Fat 4 g
- ✓ Sodium 38 mg
- ✓ Protein 5 g
- ✓ Carbohydrates 21 g
- ✓ Phosphorus 67 mg
- ✓ Fiber 1.3 g

> - ✓ Potassium 89 mg
> - ✓ Calcium 20 mg

Zucchini Turkey Burger

Total Time:

Servings: 4

Difficulty level:

Ingredients:

- Half cup minced onion
- One lengthwise sliced jalapeño pepper
- One cup shredded zucchini
- One pound ground turkey meat
- One egg
- Two fresh sliced-in-half poblano peppers
- One teaspoon Extra Spicy Blend
- One teaspoon mustard

Directions:

Step 1

Thoroughly combine extra spicy blend, onion, meat, mustard and egg.

Step 2

Create four turkey burger patties from the meat mixture. Turkey burgers can be grilled on a grill or an electric griddle outdoors.

Step 3

Grill the peppers alongside the turkey burgers until the skins are tender and blistered.

Step 4

Grill turkey burgers until they reach an interior temperature of 165° F or until no longer pink in the middle.

Step 5

Arrange sliced grilled peppers on top of the patty and end with serving on a hamburger bun.

Nutrition Facts:

Per Serving:
- Calories 211
- Cholesterol 125 mg
- Fat 10 g
- Potassium 475 mg
- Sodium 128 mg
- Protein 25 g
- Carbohydrates 5 g
- Fiber 1.6 g
- Phosphorus 280 mg
- Calcium 43 mg

Veggie Vindaloo with Naan

Total Time: 10 minutes

Servings: 6

Difficulty level: low

Ingredients:

- One-Fourth cup peeled and diced eggplant

- Two tablespoons mustard oil or canola oil
- One-Fourth cup diced zucchini
- Two diced shallots
- Half cup mixed green and red
- Six mini Indian naan bread
- One-Fourth cup cauliflower
- One cup cooked quinoa
- Two tablespoons fresh lime juice
- Two tablespoons freshly chopped cilantro
- Half cup queso fresco or paneer

Seasoning mix:

- Two teaspoons curry powder
- Half teaspoon ground cumin
- Half teaspoon turmeric
- One-Fourth teaspoon ground ginger
- One-Fourth teaspoon ground cloves
- Half teaspoon ground cinnamon
- Half teaspoon red chili pepper flakes, ground

Directions:

Step 1

Prepare the quinoa according to the package instructions.

Step 2

Combine the dry seasonings.

Step 3

Heat the oil in a large sauté pan over medium-high heat and add the eggplant, shallots, cauliflower, zucchini, and mixed peppers. Sauté for 2 to 4 minutes. Vegetables should be transparent but still crisp. Stir in the seasoning mix until well combined.

Step 4

Remove pan from stove and add cooked cilantro, lime juice, quinoa, and cheese.

Step 5

Serve cold or warm.

Nutrition Facts:

Per Serving:
- ✓ Calories 306
- ✓ Cholesterol 14 mg
- ✓ Fat 14 g
- ✓ Carbohydrates 36 g
- ✓ Phosphorus 238 mg
- ✓ Fiber 4.7 g
- ✓ Sodium 403 mg
- ✓ Protein 11 g
- ✓ Potassium 281 mg
- ✓ Calcium 158 mg

BBQ Chicken Pita Pizza

Total Time: 13 minutes

Servings: 2

Difficulty level: low

Ingredients:

- Two pita breads
- One-Fourth cup purple onion
- Three tablespoons low-sodium barbecue sauce
- Four oz. chicken, cooked
- Two tablespoons crumbled feta cheese
- One-Eighth teaspoon garlic powder

Directions:

Step 1

Preheat oven to 350° F.

Step 2

Lightly spray baking paper with non-stick cooking spray and line it with two pitas.

Step 3

Spread each pita with 1-1/2 tablespoon BBQ sauce.

Step 4

Chop onion into small pieces and spread on pitas.

Step 5

Cut chicken into cubes and spread on pitas.

Step 6

Sprinkle pitas with garlic powder and feta cheese.

Step 7

Bake 11–13 minutes.

Nutrition Facts:

> *Per Serving:*
> - ✓ Calories 320
> - ✓ Carbohydrates 37 g
> - ✓ Protein 23 g
> - ✓ Phosphorus 221 mg
> - ✓ Calcium 163 mg
> - ✓ Fat 9 g
> - ✓ Sodium 523 mg
> - ✓ Cholesterol 55 mg
> - ✓ Potassium 255 mg
> - ✓ Fiber 2.4 g

Cheesy Beef Burger

Total Time: 20 minutes

Servings: 4

Difficulty level: low

Ingredients:

- Five soda crackers (salt free)
- Three tablespoons rice milk
- One large egg
- One pound 85% lean ground beef
- One teaspoon herb seasoning blend (salt-free)

- Cheddar cheese slice

Directions:

Step 1

In a bowl, crumble the soda crackers and mix them with the milk. Allow to soak until crackers are supple.

Step 2

Beat the egg in a separate bowl and whisk it into the cracker mixture. Combine the herb blend with the crackers, breaking them up if possible. Combine the ground beef thoroughly.

Step 3

Shape the ground beef preparation into four patties of equal size.

Step 4

Grill over moderate heat until the temperature has reached at least 160° F.

Step 5

Serve on a bun with cheese slices and preferred toppings, or as a patty with your choice of vegetable and starch.

Nutrition Facts:

Per Serving:
- Calories 242
- Carbohydrates 7 g
- Protein 22 g
- Cholesterol 116 mg
- Potassium 328 mg
- Calcium 31 mg
- Fat 14 g

- ✓ Sodium 92 mg
- ✓ Phosphorus 188 mg
- ✓ Fiber 0.2 g

Savory Chicken Wraps

Total Time: 30 minutes

Servings: 4

Difficulty level: low

Ingredients:

- Eight oz. canned chicken (low-sodium)
- One stalk celery
- Half red bell pepper
- One medium carrot
- Half teaspoon onion powder
- One-Fourth cup low-fat mayonnaise
- Four 8-inch size, whole wheat tortillas

Directions:

Step 1

Chop the bell pepper, celery, and carrot into small pieces.

Step 2

In a small cup, combine the onion powder and mayonnaise.

Step 3

Top each tortilla with 1 tablespoon of the mixture.

Step 4

Mix the diced vegetables in a separate bowl.

Step 5

On one side of each flatbread, arrange ½ of the vegetables and 4 oz. chicken. If using tortillas, line one side of each tortilla with ¼ of the vegetables and 2 oz. of chicken.

Step 6

Before serving, lock each tortilla with a toothpick and slice each tortilla roll in half.

Nutrition Facts:

Per Serving:
- ✓ Calories 260
- ✓ Carbohydrates 27 g
- ✓ Protein 17 g
- ✓ Phosphorus 103 mg
- ✓ Fat 9 g
- ✓ Sodium 462 mg
- ✓ Cholesterol 42 mg
- ✓ Fiber 2.9 g
- ✓ Potassium 215 mg
- ✓ Calcium 17 mg

Shrimp Quesadill

Total Time: 10 minutes

Servings: 2

Difficulty level: low

Ingredients:

- Two tablespoons jalapeno cheddar cheese (shredded)
- One-Eighth teaspoon cayenne pepper

- Four teaspoons salsa
- Five oz. raw shrimp
- One tablespoon lemon juice
- Two tablespoons cilantro
- Two flour tortillas, burrito size
- One-Fourth teaspoon ground cumin
- Two tablespoons sour cream

Directions:

Step 1

Devein and shell the shrimp. Rinse thoroughly and slice into bite-size bits. Cut cilantro into small pieces.

Step 2

In a zip-lock container, combine the cayenne pepper, cilantro, cumin, and lemon juice to create the marinade. Set aside shrimp pieces ready to marinate.

Step 3

In a medium skillet, heat the marinade, then add the shrimp. Stir-fry for 1–2 minutes, or until the shrimp begins to turn orange. Take the skillet off the heat and spoon out the shrimp, reserving the marinade.

Step 4

Stir sour cream into the marinade in the skillet.

Step 5

In a big skillet or microwave, heat up tortillas. Each tortilla should have 2 teaspoons of salsa. Top with ½ of the shrimp mixture and 1 tablespoon of cheese.

Step 6

Spoon 1 tablespoon of the sour cream sauce on the shrimp. Fold tortilla and heat on the other side in a skillet, and then remove from pan. Do the same with the remaining shrimp, cheese, and marinade on the second tortilla.

Step 7

Divide each tortilla into four equal-sized bits. When ready to serve, sprinkle with cilantro and a lemon wedge.

Nutrition Facts:

Per Serving:

- ✓ Calories 318
- ✓ Carbohydrates 26 g
- ✓ Protein 20 g
- ✓ Phosphorus 243 mg
- ✓ Fat 15 g
- ✓ Sodium 398 mg
- ✓ Cholesterol 118 mg
- ✓ Fiber 1.2 g
- ✓ Potassium 276 mg
- ✓ Calcium 139 mg

Yummy Tacos with Mexican Seasoning

Total Time: 10 minutes

Servings: 7

Difficulty level: low

Ingredients:

- Five tablespoons sour cream
- Five tablespoons onion

- One pound ground beef
- Two cups lettuce
- Fourteen flour tortillas, 6-inch
- Half cup low-sodium tomato sauce
- Five tablespoons shredded sharp cheddar cheese

Mexican Seasoning:

- Half teaspoon garlic powder
- Two teaspoons paprika
- Three teaspoons chili powder
- One teaspoon onion powder
- Two teaspoons ground cumin
- One-Eighth teaspoon cayenne pepper

Directions:

Step 1

To prepare the Mexican Seasoning, combine all the ingredients in a small jar, set aside.

Step 2

Chop the lettuce and onion into small pieces.

Step 3

Brown the ground beef and rinse. Combine the low-sodium tomato sauce and seasoning mixture in a medium bowl. Preheat over a medium heat source. The tortillas should be warmed.

Step 4

To make soft tacos, place 1 flour tortilla on a plate and top with 1 teaspoon of cheese, 1/4 cup seasoned ground beef, 1 teaspoon of onion and lettuce to taste and 1 teaspoon of sour cream.

Nutrition Facts:

Per Serving:

- ✓ Calories 340
- ✓ Carbohydrates 32 g
- ✓ Protein 19 g
- ✓ Fat 15 g
- ✓ Sodium 494 mg
- ✓ Cholesterol 53 mg
- ✓ Potassium 422 mg
- ✓ Calcium 143 mg
- ✓ Phosphorus 276 mg
- ✓ Fiber 2.4 g

Tortilla Beef Swirls

Total Time: 10 minutes

Servings: 2

Difficulty level: low

Ingredients:

- Two flour tortillas
- Five oz. cooked roast beef
- Two tablespoons whipped cream cheese
- One-Fourth sweet bell pepper cut in strips
- One-Fourth cup chopped red onion
- Eight cucumber slices
- One teaspoon herb seasoning blend

- Two romaine lettuce leaves

Directions:

Step 1

To begin, spread cream cheese evenly over the tortillas.

Step 2

Halve the ingredients to place on two tortillas. Layer lettuce, red onion, cucumbers, pepper strips, and roast beef on each tortilla.

Step 3

Finish with a sprinkle of herb seasoning mix.

Step 4

Roll up in the manner of a jellyroll.

Step 5

Cut each tortilla in half or serve whole.

Nutrition Facts:

Per Serving:
- ✓ Calories 258
- ✓ Carbohydrates 18 g
- ✓ Protein 24 g
- ✓ Fat 10 g
- ✓ Sodium 279 mg
- ✓ Cholesterol 72 mg
- ✓ Potassium 448 mg
- ✓ Calcium 59 mg
- ✓ Phosphorus 253 mg

> ✓ Fiber 1.6 g

Chicken and Gnocchi Dumplings

Total Time: 45 minutes

Servings: 10

Difficulty level: medium

Ingredients:

- One teaspoon Italian seasoning
- Two pounds chicken breast
- One-Fourth cup grape seed or light olive oil
- One pound gnocchi
- One tablespoon low sodium Chicken Base
- Half cup finely diced fresh celery
- Six cups chicken stock (reduced-sodium)
- Half cup finely diced fresh onions
- One-Fourth cup chopped fresh parsley
- Half cup finely diced fresh carrots
- One teaspoon black pepper

Directions:

Step 1

Place a stockpot on the burner, add the oil, and switch the heat to high.

Step 2

Heat oil in a skillet and brown the chicken on all sides until lightly golden.

Step 3

Add celery, carrots, and onion. Cook, stirring occasionally, until translucent. Include chicken stock and cook for 20 to 30 minutes on high heat.

Step 4

Reduce heat to low and stir in the chicken bouillon, black pepper, and Italian seasoning. Cook, stirring continuously, for 15 minutes, adding gnocchi.

Step 5

Remove from heat, garnish with parsley, and serve.

Nutrition Facts:

Per Serving:
- Calories 362 cal
- Fat 10 g
- Cholesterol 58 mg
- Sodium 121 mg
- Carbohydrates 38 g
- Protein 28 g
- Phosphorus 295 mg
- Potassium 485 mg
- Fiber 2 g
- Calcium 38 mg

Chicken Fajita Strips

Total Time: 20 minutes

Servings: 4

Difficulty level: low

Ingredients:

- Two tablespoons lemon juice
- Eight flour tortillas
- One-Fourth cup red pepper
- One-Fourth cup green pepper
- Half cup onion
- Two tablespoons canola oil
- Half cup cilantro
- Twelve oz. boneless chicken breasts
- Two teaspoons chili powder
- One-Fourth teaspoon black pepper
- Half teaspoon cumin

Directions:

Step 1

Heat the oven to 300° F. Roll the tortillas in foil and cook for 10 minutes in the oven.

Step 2

Cut the peppers, onion, and cilantro into small pieces. Chicken breasts should be cut into 1" strips.

Step 3

In a non-stick frying pan set over medium heat, heat the oil. Add the chicken, seasonings, and lemon juice and cook for three to five minutes.

Step 4

Add peppers and onion to the frying pan and cook for an additional 3 to 5 minutes, or until the chicken has turned white and the juices run clear. Cilantro should then be added to the chicken mixture.

Step 5

Distribute chicken mixture evenly among tortillas; fold tortillas in half and serve.

Nutrition Facts:

Per Serving:
- ✓ Calories 343
- ✓ Carbohydrates 33 g
- ✓ Protein 24 g
- ✓ Cholesterol 53 mg
- ✓ Fat 13 g
- ✓ Sodium 281 mg
- ✓ Calcium 23 mg
- ✓ Phosphorus 196 mg
- ✓ Potassium 331 mg
- ✓ Fiber 2.0 g

Chicken Brunswick Broth

Total Time: 20 minutes

Servings: 6

Difficulty level: low

Ingredients:

- Two stalks celery

- One-Eighth teaspoon hot pepper sauce
- One medium onion
- Four skinless, boneless chicken breasts
- One medium red bell pepper
- One tablespoon all-purpose flour
- Two slices bacon
- One-Fourth teaspoon cayenne pepper
- One teaspoon sugar
- Eight oz. diced, canned tomatoes
- Half teaspoon Worcestershire sauce
- One cup frozen mixed vegetables
- One cup chicken broth (low-sodium)
- One tablespoon apple cider vinegar
- One bay leaf

Directions:

Step 1

Cut celery into 1/2–inch bits. Chop the bell pepper and onion into small pieces. Chicken can be cut into bite-size pieces also.

Step 2

In a large skillet over medium heat, cook the bacon until crispy. Remove bacon from pan and drain on a paper towel.

Step 3

In a medium mixing bowl, combine the cayenne pepper and flour. Toss in the raw chicken bits.

Step 4

In a medium saucepan, heat the bacon fat over medium heat. Add the chicken and cook in the reserved bacon fat. Stir periodically for approximately 4 to 6 minutes, or until lightly browned. Chicken should then be removed and set aside.

Step 5

In a saucepan, combine the celery, onion, and bell pepper. Cook and stir for approximately 4 to 5 minutes, or until the vegetables start to soften.

Step 6

Stir in the chicken broth and tomatoes. Scratch in any burnt bits and flour that have accumulated on the pan's rim.

Step 7

Combine the vinegar, cooked chicken, mixed vegetables, Worcestershire sauce, bay leaf, sugar, and hot pepper sauce in a medium mixing bowl. Crumble the bacon in the pan. Stir well to combine.

Step 8

Bring the mixture to simmer, then reduce to a low heat and cover partially. Simmer for 20 to 25 minutes, or until the broth has thickened and the vegetables are tender. Discard the bay leaf and serve immediately.

Nutrition Facts:

Per Serving:
- ✓ Protein 22 g
- ✓ Calories 172
- ✓ Calcium 39 mg
- ✓ Carbohydrates 12 g
- ✓ Cholesterol 60 mg

- ✓ Fat 4 g
- ✓ Potassium 584 mg
- ✓ Sodium 255 mg
- ✓ Phosphorus 233 mg
- ✓ Fiber 3 g

Fried Green Tomatoes

Total Time: 25 minutes

Servings: 5

Difficulty level: low

Ingredients:

- Five fresh thyme sprigs
- Three-Fourth cup cornmeal flour
- One large egg
- Two tablespoons water
- Half cup olive oil (plus more if necessary)
- Four small unripened green tomatoes (sliced)

Directions:

Step 1

Remove the thyme leaves from their stems and arrange them on a chopping board. Roll a rolling pin over the leaves to expel the oils.

Step 2

In a paper or plastic container, combine cornmeal flour, thyme, and salt (if using). Shake vigorously.

Step 3

In a small cup, crack an egg. Water should be included in this step. With a fork, beat well.

Step 4

In a large skillet, heat the olive oil over medium heat.

Step 5

Fill a floured bag halfway with 5 tomato slices. Shake vigorously to cover the tomato slices in the sauce. Repeat with the remainder of the tomato slices.

Step 6

Arrange the tomatoes with their coatings on a chopping board. Dip them in the beaten egg one at a time until well covered.

Step 7

Add moistened tomato slices one at a time to the bag to coat.

Step 8

Carefully transfer the covered tomato slices to the hot frying pan, taking care not to crowd the pan. Cook in batches to ensure enough space is around the tomatoes during the cooking process.

Step 9

Cook, for approximately 6 minutes, or until both sides are golden brown.

Step 10

Pat dry with paper towels and serve.

Nutrition Facts:

Per Serving:
- ✓ Calories 290
- ✓ Phosphorus 82 mg
- ✓ Cholesterol 37 mg

- ✓ Fat 23 g
- ✓ Fiber 2 g
- ✓ Carbohydrate 18 g
- ✓ Protein 4 g
- ✓ Calcium 18 mg
- ✓ Sodium 29 mg
- ✓ Potassium 217 mg

Savory Meat Loa

Total Time: 1 hour

Servings: 8

Difficulty level: low

Ingredients:

- One-Fourth teaspoon garlic powder
- One pound 95% lean ground beef
- Half cup chopped sweet onion
- One large egg
- Half cup bread crumbs
- Two tablespoons chopped fresh basil
- One teaspoon chopped fresh parsley
- One teaspoon chopped fresh thyme
- One tablespoon brown sugar
- One-Fourth teaspoon freshly ground black pepper
- One teaspoon white vinegar

Directions:

Step 1

Preheat oven to 350° F.

Step 2

In a large mixing bowl, combine the egg, bread crumbs, beef, onion, basil, parsley, thyme and pepper.

Step 3

Fill a 9/5 inch bread pan halfway with the meat mixture.

Step 4

Combine the brown vinegar, sugar, and garlic powder in a small cup.

Step 5

Uniformly distribute the brown sugar combination over the beef.

Step 6

Roast the meat loaf for approximately 50 minutes, or until it is thoroughly baked.

Step 7

Allow the meat loaf to rest for 10 minutes before draining any accumulated grease, then serve.

Nutrition Facts:

Per Serving:
- ✓ Calories 118
- ✓ Cholesterol 58 mg
- ✓ Fat 4 g
- ✓ Phosphorus 124 mg
- ✓ Carbohydrates 8 g

- ✓ Fiber 1 g
- ✓ Sodium 98 mg
- ✓ Protein 13 g
- ✓ Calcium 29 mg
- ✓ Potassium 231 mg

Chapter 3: Dinner

Chicken Pie Stew

Total Time: 40 minutes

Servings: 8

Difficulty level: medium

Ingredients:

- One and a half pounds fresh, skinless chicken breast
- Two cups chicken stock (low-sodium)
- One-Fourth cup canola oil
- Half cup flour
- Half cup freshly diced carrots
- Half cup freshly diced onions
- One-Fourth cup freshly diced celery
- Half teaspoon black pepper
- One tablespoon Italian seasoning (sodium-free)
- Two teaspoons Chicken Base (low sodium)

- Half cup frozen sweet peas
- Half cup heavy cream
- One cooked frozen piecrust (broken in bite-size pieces)
- One cup cheddar cheese(low-fat)

Directions:

Step 1

Preheat slow cooker at high flame for four hours.

Step 2

Heat oil in a skillet over medium heat and sauté the onions, carrots, and celery for approximately 5 minutes, or until translucent.

Step 3

Add flour and keep stirring for a further 3 minutes, or until a paste forms.

Step 4

Combine the chicken, bouillon, black pepper, Italian seasoning, and stock in a medium bowl. Stir until thoroughly combined.

Step 5

Cover and cook for approximately one hour, stirring once. Stir in the cream and peas about half hour before cooking is complete. For the final 30 minutes of cooking, cover and stir occasionally.

Step 6

To serve, garnish with piecrust bits and cheese.

Nutrition Facts:

Per Serving:
- ✓ Calories 388
- ✓ Fat 21 g

- ✓ Cholesterol 82 mg
- ✓ Sodium 424 mg
- ✓ Carbohydrates 22 g
- ✓ Protein 26 g
- ✓ Phosphorus 290 mg
- ✓ Potassium 209 mg
- ✓ Fiber 2 g
- ✓ Calcium 88 mg

Tasty Green Beans

Total Time: 5 minutes

Servings: 4

Difficulty level: low

Ingredients:

- Three-Fourth cup water
- One pound fresh green beans
- Two and a half teaspoons olive oil
- Three tablespoons fresh lemon juice
- Three fresh garlic cloves, minced
- One-Eighth teaspoon ground black pepper

Directions:

Step 1

In a large non-stick skillet, bring water to a boil; add beans and cook for 3 minutes; drain and set aside.

Step 2

In a medium-high-heat skillet, heat the oil; add the garlic and beans, and sauté for one minute.

Step 3

Add the pepper and juice and sauté for an additional minute.

Step 4

Instead of salt, use lemon juice to dig out the flavors in food. Then serve.

Nutrition Facts:

Per Serving:
- ✓ Fat 3 g
- ✓ Calories 71
- ✓ Cholesterol 0 mg
- ✓ Carbohydrates 10 g
- ✓ Sodium 2 mg
- ✓ Fiber 3.7 g
- ✓ Protein 2 g
- ✓ Potassium 186 mg
- ✓ Phosphorus 37 mg
- ✓ Calcium 55 mg

Lemon Chicken

Total Time: 3 hours

Servings: 4

Difficulty level: low

Ingredients:

- One teaspoon chopped fresh basil
- One teaspoon dried oregano
- Two minced cloves garlic
- Two tablespoons unsalted butter
- One-Fourth teaspoon ground black pepper
- One pound chicken breast
- One-Fourth cup water
- One-Fourth cup low sodium chicken broth
- One tablespoon lemon juice

Directions:

Step 1

In a small bowl, mix the black pepper and oregano and rub the chicken with the mixture.

Step 2

In a medium skillet over medium heat, melt the butter. After browning the chicken in the butter, move it to the slow cooker.

Step 3

In a pan, combine the chicken broth, sugar, lemon juice, water and garlic. Bring to a boil, stirring constantly. Then proceed to pour the sauce over the chicken.

Step 4

Cover the slow cooker and set the timer to high for 2 and a half hours, or low for five hours, depending on your preference.

Step 5

Sprinkle basil on top and baste chicken. Cover and continue cooking on high for another 15 to 30 minutes or until the chicken is juicy.

Nutrition Facts:

Per Serving:
- Calories 197
- Cholesterol 99 mg
- Fat 9 g
- Sodium 57 mg
- Protein 26 g
- Carbohydrates 1 g
- Phosphorus 251 mg
- Fiber 0.3 g
- Potassium 412 mg
- Calcium 20 mg

Sautéed Greens and Pork Chops

Total Time: 1 hour 30 minutes

Servings: 6

Difficulty level: low

Ingredients:

Smothered Pork Chops:

- One tablespoon black pepper
- Six pork loin chops
- Two teaspoons granulated onion powder
- Two teaspoons paprika
- One and a half cups fresh onions, sliced
- Two teaspoons granulated garlic powder
- Half cup canola oil
- One cup and 2 tablespoons flour
- Two cups low-sodium beef stock
- Half cup fresh scallions, sliced on the bias

Sautéed Greens:

- One-Fourth cup onions, finely diced
- One teaspoon black pepper
- Two tablespoons olive oil
- One tablespoon unsalted butter
- Eight cups fresh chopped collard greens
- One teaspoon crushed red pepper flakes
- One tablespoon chopped fresh garlic

- One teaspoon vinegar

Directions:

Preheat oven to 350° F.

Pork Chops:

Step 1

In a small bowl, combine the paprika, onion powder, black pepper, and garlic powder. Season both sides of the pork chops with half of the mixture and the other half with 1 cup of flour.

Step 2

Set aside 2 tablespoons of the flour mixture for later use.

Step 3

Brush the pork chops lightly with seasoned flour.

Step 4

On medium-high, heat the oil in a big Dutch oven.

Step 5

Fry pork chops on each side for 2–4 minutes, or until required crispness is achieved. Remove the pan from the heat and drain all but two tablespoons of the oil.

Step 6

Cook the onions for approximately 6 minutes, or until translucent. Stir in 2 tablespoons of reserved flour, ensuring it is combined well with the onions for approximately 1 minute.

Step 7

Add beef stock gradually and mix until thickened.

Step 8

Transfer pork chops to the pan and spoon sauce over them. Cook covered or wrapped in plastic, for approximately 30–45 mins at 350° F.

Step 9

Remove from oven and set aside for a minimum of 5 to 10 mins before serving.

Sautéed Greens:

Step 1

To blanch the greens, place them in a saucepan of hot water for thirty seconds.

Step 2

Remove boiling water from the strainer and quickly switch to a prepared bowl of water and ice.

Step 3

Allow to cool slightly before straining and drying the greens.

Step 4

Melt the butter and oil in a broad sauté pan over medium-high heat. Cook for approximately 4-6 minutes until the onions and garlic are slightly browned.

Step 5

Include red and black pepper and collard greens and cook, stirring continuously, for 5–8 mins on high heat.

Step 6

Remove from heat; if necessary, add vinegar and stir.

Nutrition Facts:

Per Serving:
- ✓ Calories 464
- ✓ Cholesterol 71 mg

- ✓ Fat 28 g
- ✓ Sodium 108 mg
- ✓ Protein 27 g
- ✓ Carbohydrates 26 g
- ✓ Phosphorus 289 mg
- ✓ Fiber 1.3 g
- ✓ Potassium 604 mg
- ✓ Calcium 56 mg

Stir Fried Collard Greens

Total Time: 10 minutes

Servings: 6

Difficulty level: low

Ingredients:

- Eight cups fresh chopped collard greens
- One tablespoon unsalted butter
- Two tablespoons olive oil
- One tablespoon vinegar
- One-Fourth cup finely diced onions
- One teaspoon crushed red pepper flakes
- One tablespoon chopped fresh garlic
- One teaspoon ground black pepper

Directions:

Step 1

Braise the collard greens for 30 seconds in a pan of water.

Step 2

Drain the boiling water from the greens and then move them to a big bowl of ice water. Allow to cool slightly before straining and drying the greens and setting them aside.

Step 3

Heat up the oil and butter in a broad sauté pan over medium-high heat. Cook until the onions and garlic are slightly browned, around 4–6 minutes. Fry for 5–8 minutes on high heat, stirring continuously, adding black and red pepper and collard greens.

Step 4

Remove from heat and whisk in vinegar, if necessary.

Nutrition Facts:

Per Serving:
- ✓ Calories 79 cal
- ✓ Cholesterol 5 mg
- ✓ Fat 7 g
- ✓ Potassium 129 mg
- ✓ Calcium 118 mg
- ✓ Sodium 9 mg
- ✓ Protein 2 g
- ✓ Carbohydrates 4 g
- ✓ Phosphorus 18 mg
- ✓ Fiber 2.2 g

Zesty Tilapia

Total Time: 15 minutes

Servings: 4

Difficulty level: low

Ingredients:

- Two teaspoons orange zest
- Sixteen oz. tilapia
- Three-Fourth cup celery, julienned
- One cup carrots, julienned
- Half cup green onions, sliced
- One teaspoon ground black pepper
- Four teaspoons orange juice

Directions:

Step 1

Preheat oven to 450° F.

Step 2

Combine the carrots, celery, green onions, and orange zest in a small bowl.

Step 3

Divide the tilapia into four equal parts. Remove four big sheets of foil and coat with non-stick spray.

Step 4

Arrange 14 vegetables slightly off center on each sheet of foil and cover with the fish and 1 teaspoon of orange juice. Season with freshly ground black pepper to taste.

Step 5

Fold and crimp the foil to create an envelope or pouch, and arrange the foil packs on a baking sheet. Bake for approximately 12 minutes. When done, the fish will easily separate with a fork.

Step 6

Remove the packs and immediately put them on plates. Due to the steam, exercise caution when opening.

Nutrition Facts:

Per Serving:
- Calories 133
- Cholesterol 57 mg
- Fat 2 g
- Sodium 97 mg
- Protein 24 g
- Carbohydrates 6 g
- Phosphorus 214 mg
- Dietary Fiber 1.7 g
- Potassium 543 mg
- Calcium 42 mg

Spicy Beef Stir-Fry

Total Time: 10 minutes

Servings: 4

Difficulty level: low

Ingredients:

- Two tablespoons cornstarch
- Half teaspoon sugar
- One-Fourth teaspoon sesame oil
- Two tablespoons water
- Three tablespoons canola oil
- One large beaten egg
- Twelve oz. sliced beef round tip
- One cup sliced onions
- One sliced green bell pepper
- One-Fourth teaspoon ground red chili pepper
- Two teaspoons reduced sodium soy sauce
- One tablespoon sherry
- Parsley for garnishing

Directions:

Step 1

Whisk together 1 tablespoon water, 1 tablespoon canola oil, 1 tablespoon cornstarch, and 1 large egg in a large mixing bowl. Add the beef. Allow 20 minutes for marinating.

Step 2

In a separate bowl, whisk together the remaining cornstarch and water. Set aside.

Step 3

In a pan, heat the remaining 2 tablespoons canola oil and add the meat mixture. Cook, stirring occasionally until the meat starts to brown.

Step 4

Combine the chili pepper, green bell peppers, and onion in a medium bowl. Stir in sherry and cook for 1 minute. Combine soy sauce, sugar, and sesame oil in a small bowl.

Step 5

Add water mixture and cornstarch to thicken.

Step 6

Sprinkle parsley on top of the finished beef stir-fry.

Nutrition Facts:

Per Serving:
- ✓ Calories 261
- ✓ Fat 15 g
- ✓ Cholesterol 94 mg
- ✓ Sodium 169 mg
- ✓ Carbohydrates 10 g
- ✓ Protein 21 g
- ✓ Phosphorus 167 mg
- ✓ Potassium 313 mg
- ✓ Fiber 1.5 g
- ✓ Calcium 26 mg

Herbed Rice

Total Time: 5 minutes

Servings: 6

Difficulty level: low

Ingredients:

- Two tablespoons olive oil
- Two tablespoons chopped fresh cilantro
- Four to Five cloves thinly sliced fresh garlic
- Two tablespoons chopped fresh oregano
- Three cups cooked rice
- Two tablespoons chopped fresh chives
- One teaspoon red wine vinegar
- Half teaspoon red pepper flakes

Directions:

Step 1

In a broad sauté pan over medium-high heat, heat the olive oil and slightly sauté garlic. Combine the herbs, rice, and red pepper flakes and cook for 2 to 4 minutes longer until all are well combined.

Step 2

Remove from fire, whisk in vinegar, and serve.

Nutrition Facts:

Per Serving:
- ✓ Calories 134 cal
- ✓ Cholesterol 0 mg

- ✓ Fat 5 g
- ✓ Sodium 6 mg
- ✓ Protein 2 g
- ✓ Carbohydrates 21 g
- ✓ Phosphorus 15 mg
- ✓ Dietary Fiber 1.8 g
- ✓ Potassium 56 mg
- ✓ Calcium 37 mg

Roasted Lamb Leg

Total Time: 2 hours 32 minutes

Servings: 12

Difficulty level: low

Ingredients:

- Three tablespoons lemon juice
- One 4 pound leg of lamb
- One tablespoon curry powder
- Half teaspoon ground black pepper
- Two cloves garlic, minced
- Half cup dry vermouth
- One cup onions, sliced

Directions:

Step 1

Preheat the oven to 350° F.

Step 2

Arrange lamb leg in a roasting pan with 1 teaspoon of lemon juice.

Step 3

Combine 2 teaspoons lemon juice and the remaining spices in a bowl to form a paste. The lamb should then be rubbed with the paste.

Step 4

Roast lamb for 30 minutes at 400° F.

Step 5

Remove fat from the pan and add onions and vermouth.

Step 6

Lower the heat to 325° F and continue cooking for another 1-2 hours. Regularly baste the leg of lamb. Remove from oven and allow to rest for three minutes before serving.

Nutrition Facts:

Per Serving:
- ✓ Calories 292
- ✓ Fat 20 g
- ✓ Cholesterol 86 mg
- ✓ Sodium 157 mg
- ✓ Carbohydrates 2 g
- ✓ Protein 24 g

- ✓ Phosphorus 232 mg
- ✓ Potassium 419 mg
- ✓ Dietary Fiber 0 g
- ✓ Calcium 19 mg

Skirt Steak With Bourbon Glaze

Total Time: 1 hour 30 minutes

Servings: 8

Difficulty level: medium

Ingredients:

Bourbon Glaze:

- Two tablespoons Dijon mustard
- Three tablespoons chilled unsalted butter
- One-Fourth cup diced shallots
- One cup bourbon
- One tablespoon black pepper
- One-Fourth cup dark brown sugar

Skirt Steak:

- Two pounds skirt steak
- Two tablespoons grape seed oil
- Half teaspoon dried oregano
- Half teaspoon smoked paprika
- One teaspoon black pepper
- One tablespoon red wine vinegar

Directions:

Bourbon Glaze:

Step 1

Fry the shallots in 1 tablespoon of butter in a small saucepan over medium-high heat.

Step 2

Turn down the heat to medium, remove the pan from the heat, add the bourbon, and then re-place the saucepan on the heat.

Step 3

Cook for 15 minutes, or until approximately one-third reduced.

Step 4

Whisk in the brown sugar, mustard, and black pepper until it starts bubbling.

Step 5

Remove from the heat and mix in the remaining two tablespoons of cold, cubed butter in a steady stream until fully incorporated.

Skirt Steak:

Step 1

In a gallon-size, sealable storage container, combine the first five ingredients; add steaks and shake well.

Step 2

Marinate the steaks in the pouch for 30–45 minutes at room temperature.

Step 3

Remove steaks from the bag and grill for 20 minutes on each side before removing and resting for 10 minutes.

Step 4

Cut and end with serving with a drizzle of sauce; or leave whole and brush with glaze; broil for 4–6 minutes, or until desired appearance is achieved.

Nutrition Facts:

Per Serving:
- ✓ Fat 22 g
- ✓ Calories 409
- ✓ Calcium 22 mg
- ✓ Cholesterol 93 mg
- ✓ Carbohydrates 8 g
- ✓ Sodium 152 mg
- ✓ Protein 24 g
- ✓ Potassium 283 mg
- ✓ Phosphorus 171 mg
- ✓ Fiber 0.5 g

Roast Loin Pork With Apple Stuffing

Total Time: 1 hour 30 minutes

Servings: 6

Difficulty level: medium

Ingredients:

Cherry Marmalade Glaze:

- One-Eighth teaspoon nutmeg
- Half cup sugar-free orange marmalade
- One-Fourth cup dried cherries

- One-Fourth cup apple juice
- One-Eighth teaspoon cinnamon

Apple Stuffing:

- One teaspoon black pepper
- Two cups packed cubed white read or Hawaiian rolls
- Two tablespoons butter (unsalted)
- Two tablespoons canola oil
- Half cup chicken stock (low-sodium)
- Half cup finely diced Honey Crisp apple
- One tablespoon fresh thyme
- Two tablespoons finely onions (diced)
- Two tablespoons finely celery (diced)

Roast Loin Pork:

- Two 18 inch pieces of butcher twine
- One pound boneless pork loin

Directions:

Step 1

For making Cherry Marmalade Glaze, in a small saucepan over medium-high heat, combine all glaze ingredients until the marmalade has started to melt and begins to simmer. Remove from heat.

Step 2

Preheat oven to 400° F.

Step 4

In a broad sauté pan over medium-high heat, sauté all ingredients except the chicken stock for three minutes in canola oil.

Step 5

Add chicken stock in a slow, steady stream until the mixture is moist but not too wet.

Step 6

Take the pan off the heat and cool to room temperature.

Step 7

Cut 5 slits across the length of the pork about an inch apart, creating several pockets.

Step 8

Insert approximately 2 tablespoons of stuffing into each pocket.

Step 9

Wrap one long piece of twine across the length of the loin and secure the stuffing in place with additional twine around the shorter length as required.

Step 10

Arrange leftover stuffing on a baking tray, top with bound stuffed pork, and bake at 400° F for 45 minutes, or until an interior temperature of 160° F is reached.

Step 11

Spoon the marmalade glaze over the top, turn off the oven, and leave for 10–15 minutes. Pork loin should then be removed, sliced into portions, and served.

Nutrition Facts:

> *Per Serving:*
> - ✓ Calories 263
> - ✓ Cholesterol 50 mg
> - ✓ Fat 14 g
> - ✓ Sodium 137 mg
> - ✓ Protein 14 g
> - ✓ Carbohydrates 22 g
> - ✓ Phosphorus 154 mg
> - ✓ Fiber 1 g
> - ✓ Potassium 275 mg
> - ✓ Calcium 68 mg

Rice & Cauliflower Cakes

Total Time: 30 minutes

Servings: 6

Difficulty level: low

Ingredients:

- Two cups chopped blanched cauliflower
- Olive oil for the pan
- One-Fourth cup plain yogurt
- Half cup cheddar cheese, grated
- Grounded black pepper
- Two cups cooked white basmati rice
- Two lightly beaten eggs
- One-Fourth teaspoon ground nutmeg

Directions:

Step 1

Preheat oven to 350° F.

Step 2

Coat six cups of a regular muffin tray with olive oil in a light coat.

Step 3

Combine the rice, cauliflower, milk, cheese, eggs and nutmeg in a big mixing bowl.

Step 4

Sprinkle the mixture with freshly ground pepper.

Step 5

Distribute the cauliflower mixture evenly among the six muffin cups.

Step 6

Bake for approximately 20 minutes, until it's golden and slightly puffy.

Step 7

Allow 5 minutes for them to stand before running a cutter around the corners to loosen. Serve hot, or cold.

Nutrition Facts:

Per Serving:
- ✓ Calories 161
- ✓ Cholesterol 77 mg
- ✓ Fat 6 g
- ✓ Carbohydrates 18 g
- ✓ Protein 8 g
- ✓ Fiber 1 g

- ✓ Sodium 100 mg
- ✓ Phosphorus 132 mg
- ✓ Calcium 134 mg
- ✓ Potassium 177 mg

Pork Cutlets and Sautéed Vegetable

Total Time: 20 minutes

Servings: 4

Difficulty level:

Ingredients:

- One-Eighth teaspoon black pepper
- Four 4 ounces pork cutlets
- Half teaspoon any seasoning that does not include potassium chloride
- Two tablespoons flour
- Four tablespoons margarine
- Two tablespoons fresh-squeezed lemon juice
- One third cup dry white wine
- One-Fourth teaspoon basil
- Two cups julienned zucchini
- Half cup red bell pepper
- One cup julienned yellow summer squash
- One minced clove of garlic

Directions:

Step 1

Press each cutlet to a thickness of one-fourth inches.

Step 2

Mix flour and salt-free seasoning in a mixing bowl. Cutlets should be dredged in the flour mixture.

Step 3

In a large frying pan, brown cutlets in two teaspoons of margarine for five minutes on each side.

Step 4

Transfer to a serving platter and cover with foil to keep warm.

Step 5

Combine the lemon juice and wine in the pan with the juices. Reduce to 14 cup by simmering, with 1 teaspoon of margarine stirred in.

Step 6

Spoon sauce onto cutlets and set aside to keep warm.

Step 7

In a skillet, combine the zucchini, squash, bell peppers, and 1 tablespoon of margarine.

Step 8

 Combine the garlic, basil, and black pepper in a small bowl. Sauté on high heat for 4-5 minutes.

Step 9

Arrange on a platter alongside the pork and serve.

Nutrition Facts:

Per Serving:
- ✓ Calories 403
- ✓ Cholesterol 77 mg
- ✓ Fat 32 g

- ✓ Fiber 1 g
- ✓ Carbohydrates 9 g
- ✓ Protein 20 g
- ✓ Calcium 134 mg
- ✓ Phosphorus 218 mg
- ✓ Sodium 0 mg
- ✓ Potassium 388 mg

Crispy Brussels Sprouts

Total Time: 25 minutes

Servings: 4

Difficulty level: low

Ingredients:

- Half lemon (optional)
- One lb. Brussels sprouts
- Freshly ground black pepper
- One tablespoon extra-virgin olive oil
- Two tablespoons grated parmesan cheese

Directions:

Step 1

Heat oven to 400° F.

Step 2

Trim the brown ends, and any discoloured outer leaves, from the brussels sprouts.

Step 3

Combine the brussels sprouts, olive oil, and pepper (if using) on a baking sheet and toss to cover.

Step 4

Roast for twenty minutes, tossing pan halfway through cooking. Alternatively, you can continue cooking them for an extra ten minutes for a truly crispy version.

Step 5

Drizzle with lemon juice and dust with Parmesan cheese.

Nutrition Facts:

Per Serving:
- Calories 72
- Cholesterol 0 mg
- Fat 4 g
- Carbohydrate 8 g
- Protein 3 g
- Fiber 3 g
- Sodium 25 mg
- Phosphorus 66 mg
- Calcium 42 mg
- Potassium 371 mg

Chapter 4: Desserts

Crispy Cups with Fresh Berries

Total Time: 15 minutes

Servings: 12

Difficulty level: low

Ingredients:

- One cup fresh blueberries
- Four sheets 14" x 18" phyllo dough
- One cup fresh raspberries
- Non-stick butter flavored cooking spray
- One cup fresh strawberries
- Three cups frozen dessert topping
- One cup fresh blackberries

Directions:

Step 1

Preheat oven to 400° F.

Step 2

Coat a twelve-cup pastry pan with cooking spray flavored with butter.

Step 3

Layer four sheets of phyllo dough together, gently spraying each layer with cooking spray. Create dessert cups by cutting phyllo dough into three and a half squares, and place them in a muffin tray.

Step 4

Bake for twelve minutes until the cups are golden brown. Allow to cool.

Step 5

Stuff each dessert cup halfway with fresh berries when ready to serve. Top with whipping cream for extra flavor.

Nutrition Facts:

Per Serving:
- ✓ Calories 111
- ✓ Carbohydrates 18 g
- ✓ Cholesterol 0 mg
- ✓ Protein 2 g
- ✓ Phosphorus 14 mg
- ✓ Fiber 2.6 g
- ✓ Sodium 51 mg
- ✓ Fat 4 g
- ✓ Potassium 83 mg
- ✓ Calcium 19 mg

Lemon Squares

Total Time: 40 minutes

Servings: 24

Difficulty level: low

Ingredients:

Crust:

- Two cups all-purpose flour
- Half cup powdered sugar
- One cup unsalted butter

Filling:

- Four eggs
- One-Fourth cup all-purpose flour
- One and a half cups sugar
- Half teaspoon cream of tartar
- One-Fourth cup lemon juice
- One-Fourth teaspoon baking soda

Glaze:

- Two tablespoons lemon juice
- One cup sifted powdered sugar

Directions:

Crust:

Step 1

Preheat oven to 350° F.

Step 2

Add the flour, powdered sugar, and 1 cup of softened butter in a big mixing bowl. Combine ingredients until crumbly. Press the mixture into the bottom of a 9" x 13" baking sheet.

Step 3

Bake for approximately 15–20 minutes, or until lightly browned.

Filling:

Step 4

In a medium-sized mixing bowl, lightly whisk the eggs.

Step 5

Mix the flour, cream of tartar, sugar, and baking soda in a separate bowl. Combine the dry ingredients with the eggs. Whisk in the lemon juice until the egg mixture is slightly thickened.

Step 6

Pour over the hot crust and continue baking for an additional 20 minutes, or until the filling is set.

Step 7

Remove from the oven and allow to cool.

Glaze:

Step 8

In a small cup, whisk the lemon juice and sifted powdered sugar together until spreadable. As required, adjust the amount of lemon juice.

Step 9

Spread the cooled filling on top. Allow the glaze to set before cutting into 24 bars. Refrigerate any remaining lemon bars.

Nutrition Facts:

> *Per Serving:*
> - ✓ Calories 200
> - ✓ Fat 9 g
> - ✓ Cholesterol 53 mg
> - ✓ Sodium 27 mg
> - ✓ Carbohydrates 28 g
> - ✓ Protein 2 g
> - ✓ Phosphorus 32 mg
> - ✓ Potassium 41 mg
> - ✓ Dietary Fiber 0.3 g
> - ✓ Calcium 9 mg

Pumpkin Strudel

Total Time: 30 minutes

Servings: 8

Difficulty level: low

Ingredients:

- One and a half cups sodium-free canned pumpkin (unsweetened)
- One-Eighth teaspoon nutmeg (grated)
- One teaspoon vanilla extract
- Four tablespoons sugar
- Half teaspoon cinnamon (grounded)
- Half stick butter (unsalted)
- Twelve sheets phyllo dough

Directions:

Step 1

In the center of the oven, place an oven rack. Preheat the oven to 375° F.

Step 2

In a medium-sized mixing bowl, add the nutmeg, two tablespoons sugar, canned pumpkin, vanilla extract, and 12 tablespoons of cinnamon until well mixed.

Step 3

Using a pastry brush, brush the bottom of a non-stick medium sheet dish with melted butter. On a clean board, spread a single layer of phyllo dough and cover it with butter. Then stack buttered phyllo sheets on top of one another, brushing butter onto each phyllo layer. To avoid leftover phyllo dough sheets from drying out, wrap them in cling film until ready to use.

Step 4

Once all twelve sheets have been used, spoon the mixture evenly over one of the stack's long sides. Roll from filled to unfilled end, keeping the seam side down.

Step 5

Seam-side down, transfer the roll to the oiled sheet tray, and brush with the remaining butter.

Step 6

In a small cup, combine the remaining sugar and cinnamon. Scatter it over the top and bottom of the strudel.

Step 7

Bake for approximately 12–15 minutes, or until golden brown, on the middle rack.

Step 8

Enable 10 minutes for the toasted strudel to cool before cutting with a sharp knife to allow the center to settle.

Nutrition Facts:

Per Serving:
Calories 180 cal
Cholesterol 16 mg
Fat 8 g
Sodium 141 mg
Protein 3 g
Carbohydrates 25 g
Phosphorus 39 mg
Fiber 2.0 g
Potassium 119 mg
Calcium 19 mg

Orange and Cinnamon Biscotti

Total Time: 1 hour

Servings: 18

Difficulty level: low

Ingredients:

- One-Fourth teaspoon salt
- One cup sugar
- Two large eggs
- Half cup unsalted butter
- Two teaspoons grated orange peel
- Two cups all-purpose flour
- One teaspoon vanilla extract

- One teaspoon cream of tartar
- One teaspoon ground cinnamon
- Half teaspoon baking soda

Directions:

Step 1

Preheat oven to 325° F.

Step 2

Using a non-stick cooking spray, coat two baking sheets.

Step 3

In a wide mixing bowl, combine the unsalted butter and sugar until well combined.

Step 4

Add the eggs one at a time, beating thoroughly between additions.

Step 5

Add the vanilla extract and orange peel.

Step 6

In a medium-size mixing bowl, combine baking soda, flour, cream of tartar, cinnamon, and salt.

Step 7

Stir the dry ingredients into the butter mixture until they are combined.

Step 8

Halve the dough. Each half should be placed on a prepared board. Shape each half into a three-inch-wide by three-quarters-inch-high log using lightly floured hands. Bake for approximately 35 minutes, or until the dough logs are stiff to the touch.

Step 9

Remove the dough logs from the oven and allow to cool for 10 minutes.

Step 10

Transfer logs to the work surface. Cut diagonally into 12-inch-thick slices with a serrated knife. Arrange on baking sheets, cut side down.

Step 11

Bake for approximately 12 minutes, or until the bottoms are golden.

Step 12

Turn biscotti over and bake for an additional 12 minutes, or until bottoms are golden.

Step 13

Shift to a wire rack to cool completely before serving.

Nutrition Facts:

Per Serving:
- ✓ Calories 149
- ✓ Cholesterol 34 mg
- ✓ Fat 6 g
- ✓ Sodium 76 mg
- ✓ Calcium 9 mg
- ✓ Protein 2 g
- ✓ Carbohydrates 22 g
- ✓ Potassium 53 mg
- ✓ Phosphorus 28 mg

> ✓ Fiber 0.5 g

Rustic Apple Cinnamon Filled Phyllo Pastries

Total Time: 30 minutes

Servings: 6

Difficulty level:

Ingredients:

Apple mixture:

- One package phyllo dough (6 sheets)
- 4 peeled and sliced apples
- Two tablespoons firm unsalted butter
- One-Fourth cup light brown sugar
- One-Fourth teaspoon cornstarch
- One-Fourth cup melted unsalted butter
- One-Fourth teaspoon nutmeg
- One teaspoon cinnamon
- Two tablespoons vanilla extract

mix in a bowl:

- Two tablespoons cinnamon
- Three tablespoons powdered sugar

Garnish

- Powdered sugar
- Whipped cream
- Fresh mint sprigs

Directions:

Apple mixture:

Step 1

Preheat oven to 350° F.

Step 2

Stir fry the apples in butter in a broad sauté pan over medium-high heat for 6–8 minutes.

Step 3

Combine cinnamon, nutmeg, and brown sugar in a medium bowl. Add an extra 3–4 minutes to the cooking time.

Step 4

In a small cup, whisk together the vanilla extract and cornstarch until it's fully dissolved. Fry for an extra 2 minutes on medium-high heat, stirring into the apple mixture.

Step 5

Remove from the heat and set aside mixture.

Step 6

Pastries made with phyllo dough.

Step 7

Oil a large six muffin tin pan lightly.

Step 8

Begin with the 1st sheet of phyllo dough and brush both sides with melted butter before dusting with the icing sugar and cinnamon mixture. Continue until all six sheets are buttered and dusted with the sugar and cinnamon mixture, piling each sheet on top of the previous one.

Step 9

Divide each stack into six equal squares. Cover the sides and bottom of each muffin cup with a single stack of squares, leaving a few squares hanging over the muffin cup's edges.

Step 10

Stuff each phyllo-lined muffin cup partially to 3 quarters full with the mixture of apple, ensuring that each phyllo-lined muffin cup contains an equivalent amount of apple mixture.

Step 11

In each muffin cup, fold the extra phyllo dough over the apples.

Step 12

Bake for 8–10 minutes, or until golden brown, in a preheated 350° F oven.

Step 13

Garnish with fresh mint sprigs and powdered sugar or whipped cream, if desired.

Nutrition Facts:

Per Serving:

- ✓ Calories 280
- ✓ Cholesterol 31 mg
- ✓ Fat 13 g
- ✓ Sodium 97 mg
- ✓ Protein 2 g
- ✓ Carbohydrates 38 g
- ✓ Phosphorus 33 mg
- ✓ Fiber 5 g
- ✓ Potassium 177 mg

- ✓ Calcium 44 mg

Delicious Berry Bread Pudding

Total Time: 1 hour

Servings: 10

Difficulty level: low

Ingredients:

- Whipped cream
- Eight cups challah bread (cubed)
- Two cups heavy cream
- Six beaten eggs
- One tablespoon orange zest
- Half cup sugar
- Twelve oz. bag of frozen berry medley (melted)
- Two teaspoons vanilla
- Half teaspoon cinnamon

Directions:

Step 1

Preheat oven to 375° F.

Step 2

In a large mixing bowl, whisk together the sugar, eggs, milk, vanilla, orange zest, and cinnamon until smooth.

Step 3

Using your hands, incorporate the fruit and bread cubes.

Step 4

Pour into a buttered/greased baking dish and bake for 35 minutes, filled with foil. If you're going to use butter, make sure it's unsalted.

Step 5

Remove foil and continue baking for 15 minutes longer.

Step 6

Turn the oven off and allow it to cool for ten minutes.

Step 7

Cut and serve with whipped cream on top.

Nutrition Facts:

Per Serving:
- ✓ Calories 392 cal
- ✓ Fat 23 g
- ✓ Cholesterol 189 mg
- ✓ Sodium 231 mg
- ✓ Carbohydrates 36 g
- ✓ Protein 9 g
- ✓ Phosphorus 134 mg
- ✓ Potassium 172 mg
- ✓ Fiber 2.2 g
- ✓ Calcium 65 mg

Ginger And Lemon Coconut Cookies

Total Time: 30 minutes

Servings: 12

Difficulty level: low

Ingredients:

- One cup toasted unsweetened coconut
- Half cup unsalted butter
- Half teaspoon baking soda
- One egg
- Half cup sugar
- Two tablespoons lemon juice
- One tablespoon fresh chopped and peeled ginger
- One tablespoon lemon zest
- One and a half cups flour

Directions:

Step 1

Preheat oven to 350° F.

Step 2

Scatter the coconut on a baking sheet tray and bake for around 5–10 minutes, or until the edges are light brown.

Step 3

Take the pan out of the oven and set aside.

Step 4

Using an electric mixer, combine the sugar and butter until fluffy. Then combine the egg, ginger, lemon juice, and lemon zest until smooth.

Step 5

Sift the baking soda and flour together. Combine the flour mixture and butter mixture until well combined.

Step 6

Refrigerate for at least half hour, covered.

Step 7

Scoop teaspoon-sized balls and roll in the toasted coconut. Distribute the balls evenly on a lightly oiled baking sheet pan.

Step 8

Bake for 12 minutes, or until the edges are lightly browned. Remove from the oven and cool on a counter or other cool surface before serving.

Nutrition Facts:

Per Serving:
- Calories 97
- Cholesterol 18 mg
- Fat 6 g
- Sodium 40 mg
- Protein 1 g
- Carbohydrates 11 g
- Phosphorus 17 mg
- Fiber 0.4 g
- Potassium 27 mg
- Calcium 4.4 mg

Mouth Watering Cranberry Fruit Bars

Total Time: 35 minutes

Servings: 24

Difficulty level: low

Ingredients:

Crust:

- One and a half cups all-purpose flour
- Three-Fourth cup unsalted butter
- One and a half cups sugar

Topping:

- One teaspoon baking powder
- One teaspoon vanilla extract
- Half cup all-purpose flour
- One cup dried cranberries
- Four large eggs
- Powdered sugar for dusting
- Three-Fourth cup sugar

Directions:

Step 1

Heat oven to 350° F.

Step 2

In a medium-size mixing bowl, combine the sugar and flour; slice in unsalted butter until the mixture forms a ball. Pat into a 9" x 13" baking pan that has not been greased. Bake for ten minutes, or until the tops are lightly browned.

Step 3

Sift the baking powder and flour together in a small tub. Incorporate dried cranberries. Place aside.

Step 4

In a medium-sized mixing bowl, combine the sugar, eggs, and vanilla extract. Combine flour and water. Fill baked crust halfway. Preheat oven to 200°F/180°C. Bake for 25 minutes.

Step 5

While still warm, cut into 24 bars and sprinkle with powdered sugar.

Nutrition Facts:

Per Serving:
- ✓ Calories 190
- ✓ Cholesterol 46 mg
- ✓ Fat 7 g
- ✓ Sodium 34 mg
- ✓ Protein 2 g
- ✓ Carbohydrates 31 g
- ✓ Phosphorus 34 mg
- ✓ Fiber 0.6 g
- ✓ Potassium 28 mg
- ✓ Calcium 20 mg

Minty Chocolate Brownies

Total Time: 40 minutes

Servings: 12

Difficulty level: low

Ingredients:

- Cocoa powder
- One box brownie mix
- Powdered sugar
- Twelve mint chocolates
- Fresh mint sprigs

Directions:

Step 1

Preheat oven to 350°F and make the brownie paste according to the package directions.

Step 2

Line and flour the bottom layer of a 12-cup muffin pan. After pouring the brownie batter into the prepared pans, bake for 30 minutes.

Step 3

Take the brownies from the oven and insert one slice of mint candy in the middle of each, then bake for an extra five minutes. Switch off and remove the oven. Allow 5–10 minutes for cooling.

Step 4

Carefully remove the brownie cupcakes from the pan and serve.

Step 5

Garnish with cocoa powder, fresh mint and powdered sugar, if desired.

Nutrition Facts:

Per Serving:

- ✓ Calories 307
- ✓ Cholesterol 32 mg
- ✓ Fat 18 g
- ✓ Potassium 120 mg
- ✓ Sodium 147 mg
- ✓ Protein 3 g
- ✓ Carbohydrates 36 g
- ✓ Fiber 0 g
- ✓ Phosphorus 61 mg
- ✓ Calcium 23 mg

Sugar And Cream Cheese Cookies

Total Time: 2 hours 10 minutes

Servings: 24

Difficulty level: low

Ingredients:

- Two and One-Fourth cups all-purpose flour
- One cup sugar
- Three oz softened cream cheese
- Half teaspoon vanilla extract
- One cup unsalted butter (softened)
- One large egg
- One-Fourth teaspoon almond extract

- Half teaspoon salt

Directions:

Step 1

Combine the butter, sugar, almond extract, salt, vanilla extract, cream cheese, and egg yolk in a big mixing bowl. Blend thoroughly. Incorporate flour until well-combined.

Step 2

Refrigerate cookie dough for two hours.

Step 3

Heat oven to 350° F.

Step 4

Spread out the dough, one third at a time, to a 14-inch thickness on a lightly floured surface. Cut with cookie cutters into ideal shapes.

Step 5

Arrange them on an ungreased cookie tray 1 inch apart. Leave the cookies as they are, or brush with a lightly beaten egg white and top with sugar, if desired.

Step 6

Bake for 7 to 9 minutes, or until they are a light golden brown. Cream cheese cookies. Before serving, allow to cool fully.

Nutrition Facts:

Per Serving:
- ✓ Calories 79
- ✓ Cholesterol 16 mg
- ✓ Fat 5 g
- ✓ Sodium 33 mg

- ✓ Protein 1 g
- ✓ Carbohydrates 9 g
- ✓ Phosphorus 11 mg
- ✓ Fiber 0 g
- ✓ Potassium 11 mg
- ✓ Calcium 4 mg

Lemon Cupcakes

Total Time: 30 minutes

Servings: 33

Difficulty level: low

Ingredients:

- Non-stick cooking spray
- One box angel food cake mix
- Two tablespoons water
- One box lemon cake mix

Directions:

Step 1

Pour the angel food cake mix and lemon cake mix into a big plastic bag fitted with a zip lock. Combine the 2 dry cake mixes in the sealed plastic container. You can make a batch of cupcakes or a single cupcake, depending on your preference.

Step 2

Using non-stick cooking spray, coat a small custard dish.

Step 3

Put three tablespoons of dry cake mix in an oiled custard dish.

Step 4

Mix in two tablespoons of water.

Step 5

Cook for one minute on high in the microwave.

Step 6

Remove the cupcake from the custard bowl. Allow one minute to cool before serving.

Nutrition Facts:

Per Serving:
- ✓ Calories 97
- ✓ Carbohydrates 21 g
- ✓ Protein 1 g
- ✓ Fat 1 g
- ✓ Sodium 163 mg
- ✓ Cholesterol 0 mg
- ✓ Potassium 17 mg
- ✓ Calcium 21 mg
- ✓ Phosphorus 80 mg
- ✓ Fiber 0 g

Blueberry and Apple Crisp

Total Time: 1 hour

Servings: 8

Difficulty level: low

Ingredients:

Crisp

- Six tablespoons melted non-hydrogenated margarine
- 310 ml rolled oats (quick cooking)
- One-Fourth cup all-purpose flour (unbleached)
- One-Fourth cup brown sugar

Filling

- One tablespoon lemon juice
- One tablespoon melted margarine
- Half cup brown sugar
- Four cups fresh or frozen blueberries
- Four teaspoons cornstarch
- Two cups chopped apples

Directions:

Step 1

Preheat oven to 350°F with the rack in the centre spot.

Step 2

In a separate cup, whisk together the dry ingredients. Stir in the butter until just moistened. Place aside.

Step 3

Mix the cornstarch and brown sugar in a 8-inch square baking dish. Toss in the lemon juice and fruits.

Step 4

Bake for 1 hour, or until the crisp is nicely browned. Serve at room temperature or chilled.

Nutrition Facts:

Per Serving:
- ✓ Calories 318
- ✓ Carbohydrates 52 g
- ✓ Protein 3.3 g
- ✓ Fiber 4 g
- ✓ Sodium 148 mg
- ✓ Fat 12 g
- ✓ Phosphorus 93 mg
- ✓ Cholesterol 0 mg
- ✓ Potassium 196 mg
- ✓ Calcium 21 mg

Chapter 5: Beverages

Lemonade

Total Time: 10 minutes

Servings: 10

Difficulty level: low

Ingredients:

- Two and a half cups water
- Half teaspoon finely shredded lemon
- One and one-fourth cups sugar
- Ice cubes
- One and one-fourth cups lime juice

Directions:

Step 1

In a medium saucepan over medium heat, stir the water and sugar together until the sugar is dissolved. Remove from heat and allow to cool for 20 minutes.

Step 2

To the sugar mixture, add the citrus peel and juice. Fill a jug halfway with the mixture; cover and cool.

Step 3

In ice-filled containers, combine three oz. base and three ounces water for each glass of lemonade. To relax, stir and drink slowly. Freeze any remaining base in an ice cube container and use in place of ice in drinks.

Nutrition Facts:

Per Serving
- ✓ Calories 108
- ✓ Carbohydrates 27 g
- ✓ Protein 0 g
- ✓ Fat 0 g
- ✓ Sodium 2 mg
- ✓ Cholesterol 0 mg
- ✓ Potassium 39 mg
- ✓ Calcium 4 mg
- ✓ Phosphorus 2 mg
- ✓ Fiber 0.1 g

Apple Cinnamon Cider

Total Time: 3 hours 20 minutes

Servings: 1

Difficulty level: low

Ingredients:

- One tablespoon ground cinnamon
- Ten apples
- One tablespoon ground all spice
- Half cup white sugar
- Nutmeg
- Star anise
- Ginger

Directions:

Step 1

In a big stockpot, combine apples and enough water to cover by at least two inches.

Step 2

Combine the cinnamon, sugar, and all spice in a medium bowl. Increase the heat to high and bring to a simmer. Boil for 1 hour, uncovered.

Step 3

Cover the oven, reduce to a low heat, and cook for 2 hours.

Step 4

Using a fine mesh sieve, strain the apple mixture. Solids should be discarded. Cider should be drained once more through a cheesecloth-lined sieve. Refrigerate until fully chilled. This recipe can also be made in the crockpot.

Nutrition Facts:

Per Serving:
- ✓ Fat 0.3g
- ✓ Sodium 9.9mg
- ✓ Cholesterol 0mg
- ✓ Calcium 4 mg
- ✓ Fiber 0.5g
- ✓ Carbohydrate 28g
- ✓ Protein 0.2g
- ✓ Phosphorus 17.4mg
- ✓ Potassium 250.5mg
- ✓ Calories 114

Chocolate Smoothie

Total Time: 2 minutes

Servings: 4

Difficulty level: low

Ingredients:

- One-Fourth cup condensed milk
- Two tablespoons liqueur
- Pinch of nutmeg
- Half cup evaporated milk
- Two scoops chocolate-flavored whey protein
- Two cups ice
- One-Fourth teaspoon ground cinnamon

Directions:

Step 1

In a blender, combine all the ingredients except the cinnamon on high speed until smooth, for around 1-2 minutes.

Step 2

Garnish with cinnamon and whipped cream.

Nutrition Facts:

Per Serving:
- ✓ Calories 142
- ✓ Cholesterol 18 mg
- ✓ Fat 4 g
- ✓ Sodium 134 mg
- ✓ Protein 10 g
- ✓ Carbohydrates 17 g
- ✓ Phosphorus 162 mg
- ✓ Fiber 0.9 g
- ✓ Potassium 247 mg
- ✓ Calcium 204 mg

Blueberry Smoothie

Total Time: 5 minutes

Servings: 1

Difficulty level: low

Ingredients:

- One cup rice milk
- One-Fourth cup frozen blueberries
- One teaspoon honey or sugar
- Ice cubes
- One sprig fresh mint

Directions:

Step 1

In a blender, puree the rice milk, blueberries, mint, sugar, and additional ice. Serve immediately in a tall bottle.

Nutrition Facts:

Per Serving:

- ✓ Fat 0.5g
- ✓ Sodium 28.1mg
- ✓ Cholesterol 0mg
- ✓ Carbohydrate 16.5g
- ✓ Potassium 29.7mg
- ✓ Fiber 1.1g
- ✓ Phosphorus 21.2mg
- ✓ Protein 10 g

- ✓ Calories 70
- ✓ Calcium 204 mg

Masala Chai Tea

Total Time: 30 minutes

Servings: 8

Difficulty level: low

Ingredients:

- Half cup brown sugar
- Six cups water
- Two and a half cups rice milk
- One and a half cup heavy whipping cream
- Two tablespoons black tea leaves
- Two black peppercorns
- Two cinnamon sticks
- Ten whole cloves
- Three star anise
- Six cardamom pods
- Three whole nutmeg

Directions:

Step 1

Combine the spices and 1 cup of water in a 2-quart saucepan. Bring to a simmer; remove from heat; steep for twenty minutes, depending on the intensity of the spice flavour desired.

Step 2

To the water and spices, add cream and rice milk. Decrease the spice mixture and cream to a low boil and immediately remove from the oven.

Step 3

Add the mixture to the milk and steep for 5 to 10 minutes, or until desired flavor is achieved. At this stage, you can either add sugar or serve without it. Sugar is traditionally added only before serving.

Step 4

Strain into a saucepan. Season with sugar to taste. Serve.

Nutrition Facts:

Per Serving:
- Fat 8.7 g
- Fiber 1.3 g
- Sodium 28.2 mg
- Carbohydrate 17.6 g
- Potassium 85.1 mg
- Calcium 0.6 mg
- Calories 145
- Phosphorus 24.5 mg
- Cholesterol 25.4 mg
- Protein 1 g

Apple And Beet Juice

Total Time: 5 minutes

Servings: 2

Difficulty level: low

Ingredients:

- One medium apple
- One-fourth cup parsley
- One medium fresh carrot
- Half medium beet
- One celery stalk

Directions:

Step 1

In a juicer, combine the beet, apple, celery, carrot, and parsley.

Step 2

Divide between two glasses to make two servings. Consume immediately, or chill in the refrigerator.

Nutrition Facts:

Per Serving:
- ✓ Protein 1 g
- ✓ Calories 53
- ✓ Carbohydrates 13 g
- ✓ Cholesterol 0 mg
- ✓ Fat 0 g
- ✓ Fiber 0 g

- ✓ Sodium 66 mg
- ✓ Phosphorus 36 mg
- ✓ Potassium 338 mg
- ✓ Calcium 36 mg

Fabulous Hot Cocoa

Total Time: 10 minutes

Servings: 1

Difficulty level: low

Ingredients:

- One cup very hot water
- Two teaspoons granulated sugar
- One tablespoon unsweetened cocoa powder
- Three tablespoons whipped cream
- Two tablespoons cold water

Directions:

Step 1

One cup of water should be heated.

Step 2

In a cup, combine the sugar and cocoa powder while the water is heating.

Step 3

Combine with cold water to create a thin paste.

Step 4

Fill the cup halfway with hot water. To remove the paste, stir well.

Step 5

Serve with whipped cream on top.

Nutrition Facts:

Per Serving:
- ✓ Calories 72
- ✓ Cholesterol 0 mg
- ✓ Carbohydrates 13 g
- ✓ Protein 1 g
- ✓ Fat 3 g
- ✓ Sodium 10 mg
- ✓ Potassium 100 mg
- ✓ Calcium 26 mg
- ✓ Phosphorus 49 mg
- ✓ Fiber 1.8 g

Chocolate Shake

Total Time: 5 minutes

Servings: 1

Difficulty level: low

Ingredients:

- Chocolate bar shavings
- One tablespoon powdered unsweetened cocoa
- One tablespoon sugar
- One tablespoon cold water

- Four tablespoons whipped topping
- Eight oz. pasteurized liquid egg white

Directions:

Step 1

Combine the cold water, cocoa, and sugar in a mixing bowl.

Step 2

Continue stirring until the sugar dissolves.

Step 3

Combine the egg whites and three tablespoons of whipped topping. Stir until the whipped topping is totally melted.

Step 4

Garnish with shaved chocolate bars and one tablespoon whipped topping.

Nutrition Facts:

Per Serving:
- ✓ Calories 215
- ✓ Carbohydrates 18 g
- ✓ Protein 29 g
- ✓ Fat 3 g
- ✓ Sodium 430 mg
- ✓ Cholesterol 0 mg
- ✓ Potassium 503 mg
- ✓ Calcium 26 mg
- ✓ Phosphorus 78 mg

> ✓ Fiber 1.8 g

Pineapple Protein Smoothie

Total Time: 5 minutes

Servings: 1

Difficulty level: low

Ingredients:

- Three-Fourth cup pineapple sherbet
- Half cup water
- One scoop vanilla whey protein powder
- Two ice cubes

Directions:

Step 1

Combine the whey protein powder, pineapple sherbet, and water in a blender. You can add ice cubes if you want.

Step 2

Blend instantly for 45 seconds and serve.

Nutrition Facts:

> *Per Serving:*
> ✓ Calories 268
> ✓ Carbohydrates 40 g
> ✓ Protein 18 g
> ✓ Fat 4 g
> ✓ Sodium 93 mg

- ✓ Cholesterol 36 mg
- ✓ Potassium 237 mg
- ✓ Calcium 160 mg
- ✓ Phosphorus 160 mg
- ✓ Fiber 1.4 g

Fruity Smoothie

Total Time: 5 minutes

Servings: 2

Difficulty level: low

Ingredients:

- One cup crushed ice
- Eight oz. Canned fruit cocktail with juice inside
- One cup cold water
- Two scoops of vanilla flavored whey protein powder

Directions:

Step 1

In a blender, combine all the ingredients.

Step 2

Divide the mixture into two parts and serve.

Nutrition Facts:

Per Serving:
- ✓ Calories 186
- ✓ Carbohydrates 19 g

- ✓ Protein 23 g
- ✓ Fat 2 g
- ✓ Sodium 62 mg
- ✓ Cholesterol 41 mg
- ✓ Potassium 282 mg
- ✓ Calcium 160 mg
- ✓ Phosphorus 118 mg
- ✓ Fiber 1.1 g

Snow Cone Smoothie

Total Time: 5 minutes

Servings: 1

Difficulty level: low

Ingredients:

- Eight oz. pasteurized liquid egg white
- One teaspoon liquid strawberry flavor enhancing drops
- Three tablespoons dairy whipped topping

Directions:

Step 1

In a soda shaker, combine all the ingredients.

Step 2

Shake vigorously until all of the whipped topping has melted.

Step 3

If needed, add ice. Serve and drink with pleasure!

Nutrition Facts:

Per Serving:

- ✓ Calories 118
- ✓ Carbohydrates 4 g
- ✓ Protein 21 g
- ✓ Fat 2 g
- ✓ Sodium 411 mg
- ✓ Cholesterol 8 mg
- ✓ Potassium 389 mg
- ✓ Calcium 32 mg
- ✓ Phosphorus 38 mg
- ✓ Fiber 0 g

Cinnamon and Hazelnut Coffee

Total Time: 5 minutes

Servings: 4

Difficulty level: low

Ingredients:

- Four cups brewed coffee
- Four cinnamon sticks
- Four tablespoons 1% low fat milk
- Eight teaspoons Classic Hazelnut Syrup (Sugar Free)

Directions:

Step 1

In a coffee machine, brew the coffee. Fill medium cups halfway.

Step 2

To each cup, add one tablespoon of milk and two teaspoons of the classic hazelnut syrup and garnish with a cinnamon stick.

Nutrition Facts:

Per Serving
- Calories 13
- Carbohydrates 1 g
- Protein 1 g
- Fat 0 g
- Sodium 13 mg
- Cholesterol 1 mg
- Potassium 139 mg
- Calcium 24 mg
- Phosphorus 22 mg
- Fiber 0 g

Spiced Eggnog

Total Time: 2 minutes

Servings: 6

Difficulty level: low

Ingredients:

- Two cups half & half creamer
- Three-Fourth cup egg product (low cholesterol)

- One-Fourth cup sugar
- Two teaspoons rum extract
- Half teaspoon pumpkin pie spice
- One-Fourth teaspoon nutmeg
- Six tablespoons whipped cream

Directions:

Step 1

In a chilled blender, mix the egg product, rum extract, half & half creamer, sugar, and pumpkin pie spice and process for 1 to 2 minutes.

Step 2

Divide among six small glasses. Each serving should be garnished with a tablespoon of whipped topping and a pinch of nutmeg.

Nutrition Facts:

Per Serving:
- Calories 162
- Carbohydrates 13g
- Protein 5 g
- Fat 10 g
- Sodium 78 mg
- Cholesterol 32 mg
- Potassium 149 mg
- Calcium 99 mg
- Phosphorus 83 mg
- Fiber 0 g

Chapter 6: Soups

Sweet Cherry Soup

Total Time: 15 minutes

Servings: 4

Difficulty level: low

Ingredients:

- One and a half cups fresh cherries
- Three cups water
- One third cup sugar
- Salt to taste
- One tablespoon all-purpose white flour
- Half cup sour cream (reduced-fat)

Directions:

Step 1

Cherry pits should be removed.

Step 2

In a medium sauce pan, combine the water, cherries, sugar, and salt. Bring to a boil and then reduce to a very low heat and continue to cook for 10 minutes.

Step 3

Reserve 2 teaspoons of liquid for garnish.

Step 4

Strain one-fourth cup of the liquid and set aside to cool slightly.

Step 5

Whisk in the sour cream and flour until combined, then switch to the sauce pan.

Step 6

Continue simmering for an additional five minutes over medium heat.

Step 7

Take the pan off the heat and leave to cool.

Step 8

Ladle into soup bowls. As a garnish, drizzle in the preserved cherry juice and serve.

Nutrition Facts:

Per Serving:
- Calories 144
- Carbohydrates 25 g
- Protein 2 g
- Fat 4 g
- Sodium 57 mg
- Cholesterol 12 mg

- ✓ Potassium 144 mg
- ✓ Calcium 47 mg
- ✓ Phosphorus 40 mg
- ✓ Fiber 1.0

Chicken Noodle Soup

Total Time: 30 minutes

Servings: 10

Difficulty level: low

Ingredients:

- One prepared rotisserie chicken
- Half cup onion
- Eight cups chicken broth (low-sodium)
- One cup celery
- Six oz. wide uncooked noodles
- One cup carrots
- Three tablespoons fresh parsley

Directions:

Step 1

De-bone the chicken and cut into bite-size pieces. For the broth, measure 4 cups.

Step 2

In a big stock pot, pour in the chicken broth and bring to a boil.

Step 3

Chop the onion and celery.

Step 4

In a stock pot, combine the chicken, vegetables, and noodles.

Step 5

Bring to a boil and cook, stirring occasionally, for approximately 15 minutes, or until noodles are tender.

Step 6

Garnish with parsley, if desired and serve.

Nutrition Facts:

Per Serving:
- ✓ Calories 185
- ✓ Carbohydrates 14 g
- ✓ Protein 21 g
- ✓ Fat 5 g
- ✓ Sodium 361 mg
- ✓ Cholesterol 63 mg
- ✓ Potassium 294 mg
- ✓ Calcium 22 mg
- ✓ Fiber 1.4 g
- ✓ Phosphorus 161 mg

Gnocchi and Chicken Dumplings

Total Time: 15 minutes

Servings: 10

Difficulty level: low

Ingredients:

- Two lb. chicken breast
- One-Fourth cup grape seed or light olive oil
- One pound gnocchi
- One teaspoon Italian seasoning
- One tablespoon low sodium Chicken Base
- Half cup finely diced fresh celery
- Six cups reduced-sodium chicken stock
- Half cup finely diced fresh onions
- One-Fourth cup chopped fresh parsley
- Half cup finely diced fresh carrots
- One teaspoon black pepper

Directions:

Step 1

Place a stockpot on the burner, add the oil, and switch the heat to high.

Step 2

Heat the oil in a skillet and brown the chicken on all sides until nicely browned.

Step 3

Add the celery, carrots, and onion and cook, stirring occasionally, until translucent. Add stock of chicken and cook for half hour on high heat.

Step 4

Reduce the heat to low and stir in the chicken bouillon, black pepper, and Italian seasoning. Cook, stirring continuously for fifteen minutes, adding gnocchi.

Step 5

Remove from heat, garnish with parsley, and serve.

Nutrition Facts:

Per Serving:
- Calories 362
- Cholesterol 58 mg
- Fat 10 g
- Sodium 121 mg
- Protein 28 g
- Carbohydrates 38 g
- Phosphorus 295 mg
- Fiber 2 g
- Potassium 485 mg
- Calcium 38 mg

Carrot and Cabbage Soup

Total Time: 55 minutes

Servings: 8

Difficulty level: low

Ingredients:

- One tablespoon olive oil
- Two teaspoons minced garlic

- Half chopped sweet onion
- Six cups water
- Half head shredded green cabbage
- One cup sodium-free chicken stock
- Two carrots, diced
- Black pepper to taste
- Two medium diced tomatoes
- Two tablespoons chopped fresh thyme

Directions:

Step 1

Preheat the olive oil in a large pan over medium heat.

Step 2

Add the garlic and onion then sauté for approximately three minutes, or until softened.

Step 3

Bring to a simmer with the chicken stock, water, carrots, cabbage, and tomatoes. Reduce to a medium-low heat and continue cooking for approximately 30 minutes, or until the veggies are tender.

Step 4

Sprinkle the soup with freshly ground black pepper. Serve immediately, garnished with thyme.

Nutrition Facts:

Per Serving:
- ✓ Calories 58
- ✓ Carbohydrates 8 g

- ✓ Calcium 47 mg
- ✓ Fat 3g
- ✓ Protein 2g
- ✓ Phosphorus 40 mg
- ✓ Cholesterol 0 mg
- ✓ Sodium 45 mg
- ✓ Potassium 245 mg

Vegetable Soup

Total Time: 1 hour

Servings: 10

Difficulty level: low

Ingredients:

- One and a half litres water
- One medium onion
- One medium turnip
- Six large carrots
- Two sticks celery
- vegetable or chicken low salt stock cubes
- Two large garlic cloves
- One bay leaf
- One-Fourth teaspoon black pepper
- One teaspoon chopped fresh thyme
- One tablespoon olive oil

Directions:

Step 1

Peel and finely chop the carrot, onion, and turnip.

Step 2

Cut the celery and garlic finely.

Step 3

In a big pot, combine the carrots and turnips with four times their amount of water. Bring to a simmer and cook until they are tender.

Step 4

Preheat the olive oil in a heavy-bottomed saucepan while the carrots and turnips cook.

Step 5

Add the celery, garlic, and onion to the hot oil. With a spoon, coat the vegetables in the oil.

Step 6

Cover the pan and set it to a medium heat to half-fry until the vegetables are softened. This process should take approximately 15 minutes.

Step 7

Shake the pot occasionally and stir to ensure that nothing burns or sticks.

Step 8

Once cooked, stir in the boiled carrots and turnips.

Step 9

Make vegetable or chicken stock by combining one very low sodium chicken or vegetable stock cube with 1 to 1.2 litres of boiling water.

Step 10

Distribute the stock evenly over the vegetable mixture.

Step 11

Combine the thyme and bay leaf in a small bowl.

Step 12

Season with freshly ground pepper.

Step 13

Bring to a boil and then reduce to a low heat and simmer for 30 minutes with the lid off.

Step 14

Discard the bay leaf.

Step 15

Puree the soup in a liquidizer until smooth.

Step 16

At this stage, additional water can be added to achieve a thinner soup, depending on your preference.

Nutrition Facts:

Per Serving:
- ✓ Calories 42
- ✓ Fat 1.6g
- ✓ Carbohydrate 5.7g
- ✓ Calcium 38 mg
- ✓ Cholesterol 58 mg
- ✓ Protein 1g
- ✓ Potassium 3.3mg
- ✓ Sodium 0.1g
- ✓ Phosphorus 23mg

✓ Fiber 2 g

Minestrone Soup

Total Time: 45 minutes

Servings: 4

Difficulty level:

Ingredients:

- One can green snap beans
- Fourteen oz. diced tomatoes
- Four cups chicken broth (Low Sodium)
- One and a half cups elbow shaped macaroni
- Half large onion
- One teaspoon ground black pepper
- One teaspoon basil leaves
- One teaspoon oregano leaves
- Half cup zucchini (chopped)
- Two large celery stalks
- One large carrot
- Two garlic cloves
- Two tablespoons olive oil

Directions:

Step 1

Cut the garlic, onion, and zucchini into small cubes. The carrot should be shredded. Rinse the green beans and cut into half inch pieces.

Step 2

In a large saucepan or Dutch oven, heat olive oil over medium heat. Cook for 2-3 minutes, or until the onions are translucent.

Step 3

Combine the garlic, carrot, celery, and zucchini in a medium bowl. (If using new green beans, add them). Cook for approximately 5 minutes, or until the vegetables are tender.

Step 4

Combine the green beans, oregano, basil, and black pepper in a medium bowl.

Step 5

Combine one can of diced, no-salt chicken broth and tomatoes in a medium bowl.

Step 6

Bring to a simmer and reduce to a low heat. Cook for ten minutes.

Step 7

Include pasta and cook for ten minutes, or until al dente, as directed on the box.

Step 8

Garnish with a new basil sprig. Spoon into a bowl and serve immediately!

Nutrition Facts:

Per Serving:
- ✓ Calories 144
- ✓ Fiber 2.8 g
- ✓ Carbohydrates 21.9 g
- ✓ Protein 5.9 g
- ✓ Fat 4.3 g
- ✓ Sodium 55.1 mg

- ✓ Calcium 51.3 mg
- ✓ Potassium 355.2 mg
- ✓ Phosphorus 97.8 mg

Apple Soup and Smoked Chicken

Total Time: 1 hour 5 minutes

Servings: 4

Difficulty level: low

Ingredients:

- One lb. of boneless chicken breast
- One tablespoon canola oil
- Four stalks diced celery
- One diced onion
- One teaspoon sugar
- Three peeled and diced apples
- Half teaspoon sage (dried)
- One teaspoon ground thyme
- Four cups low sodium chicken stock
- One and a half teaspoons horseradish
- Half teaspoon liquid smoke
- One teaspoon apple cider vinegar

Directions:

Step 1

Sauté the oil, onions, celery, and apples in a stock pot over medium heat until the onions become translucent.

Step 2

After one minute, add the sage and thyme.

Step 3

In a medium cup, combine liquid smoke, chicken stock, vinegar, horseradish, and sugar.

Step 4

Reduce to a low heat and continue simmering for ten minutes.

Step 5

At this point, blend the soup using a blender.

Step 6

Stir in the diced chicken and cook for an additional ten minutes, or until the chicken is cooked through.

Nutrition Facts:

Per Serving:
- ✓ Sodium 150 mg
- ✓ Calories 194
- ✓ Fiber 3.5 g
- ✓ Carbohydrates 17 g
- ✓ Phosphorus 188 mg
- ✓ Protein 20.1 g
- ✓ Cholesterol 6 mg
- ✓ Potassium 600 mg
- ✓ Fat 4.5 g
- ✓ Calcium 30 mg

Chicken Noodle Soup

Total Time: 50 minutes

Servings: 4

Difficulty level: low

Ingredients:

- One tablespoon margarine or butter
- Half teaspoon garlic powder
- Half diced onion
- Half cup sliced carrots
- Two diced celery stalks
- Three cups low sodium chicken broth
- Eight oz. boiled shredded chicken breast
- One cup water
- Ten oz. egg noodles
- Half teaspoon oregano
- Half teaspoon basil
- One-Fourth teaspoon pepper

Directions:

Step 1

In a big saucepan, melt butter.

Step 2

Combine the celery, onion, and carrots in a medium bowl.

Step 3

Cook in the pan until the onions are translucent.

Step 4

Combine the water, chicken, chicken broth, and noodles.

Step 5

Increase heat to high and bring to a simmer.

Step 6

Reduce to a low heat.

Step 7

Incorporate herbs. Cook on low heat for 20 minutes. Have fun!

Nutrition Facts:

Per Serving:
- Calories 182
- Cholesterol 6 mg
- Fiber 1.6 g
- Protein 11.9 g
- Carbohydrates 25.3 g
- Phosphorus 108 mg
- Fat 3.8 g
- Calcium 24 mg
- Sodium 85 mg
- Potassium 210 mg

Tuscan Vegetable Soup

Total Time: 10 minutes

Servings: 6

Difficulty level: low

Ingredients:

- One tablespoon Shredded Parmesan cheese
- One tablespoon olive oil
- One and a half teaspoon dried thyme
- One and a half cups chopped onion
- Four cups green chopped cabbage
- Three teaspoons minced garlic
- One 14.5 oz. can tomatoes
- Two cups diced carrots
- Two cups sliced celery
- One 15 oz. can red kidney beans or white kidney beans
- Eight cups low sodium chicken or vegetable broth
- Half cup chopped basil
- Three cups diced potato
- Three cups diced zucchini

Directions:

Step 1

In a large non-stick saucepan, heat olive oil over medium heat. Sauté the thyme, onion, and garlic for approximately 5 minutes.

Step 2

Add the cabbage pieces, celery, stewed tomato sauce, carrots and sauté for a further 8-10 minutes. Put to a boil the fresh basil, chicken broth, zucchini, potatoes, and kidney beans. Reduce heat to low, cover the saucepan, and allow to simmer for approximately one hour.

Step 3

Pour into serving bowls and garnish with a tablespoon of Parmesan cheese for each serving.

Nutrition Facts:

Per Serving:
- ✓ Calories 137
- ✓ Carbohydrates 24 g
- ✓ Protein 7.6 g
- ✓ fiber 5.3 g
- ✓ Fat 2.7 g
- ✓ Cholesterol 0.3 mg
- ✓ Calcium 79.6 mg
- ✓ Sodium 272 mg
- ✓ Potassium 718 mg

Carrot and Ginger Soup

Total Time: 20 minutes

Servings: 3

Difficulty level: low

Ingredients:

- One-Fourth teaspoon roasted sesame seed oil
- Half teaspoon canola oil
- Two tablespoons sliced fresh ginger
- Four diced carrots
- Half teaspoon minced garlic
- One diced shallot
- Two cups low-sodium chicken stock
- Half teaspoon horseradish
- Two teaspoons white vinegar
- Six ounces Tofu
- Four drops low sodium soy sauce
- One teaspoon sugar

Directions:

Step 1

In a medium sauce pan combine the oil, ginger, carrots, and shallots.

Step 2

Cook over medium heat, stirring occasionally, until the carrots are soft. Continue cooking for a further 2 minutes with the garlic and horseradish.

Step 3

Simmer for 15 minutes with crushed tofu and chicken stock.

Step 4

Combine the sugar, vinegar, and low-sodium soy sauce in a small bowl. In a blender, puree the broth. Distribute the soup among the bowls and pour sesame seed oil over the top of each.

Nutrition Facts:

Per Servings:
- ✓ Calories 129
- ✓ Cholesterol 3.3 MG
- ✓ Fat 2.9 G
- ✓ Calcium 67 MG
- ✓ Phosphorus 112 MG
- ✓ Sodium 239 MG
- ✓ Potassium 566 MG
- ✓ Fiber 3.7 G
- ✓ Carbohydrates 16.5 G
- ✓ Protein 8.4 G

Parsnip and Pear Soup

Total Time: 1 hour 30 minutes

Servings: 4

Difficulty level: low

Ingredients:

- Two cups chopped parsnips
- One-Fourth teaspoon sea salt
- One tablespoon olive oil
- One-Eighth teaspoon black pepper
- Three-Fourth teaspoon ground nutmeg
- One large chopped pear
- One medium leek thinly sliced
- Two tablespoons unsalted butter
- One small sliced pear
- One stalk celery, chopped
- Three cups (low sodium) vegetable broth
- Half cup chopped onion
- One tablespoon honey
- Two teaspoons minced rosemary leaves
- One bay leaf
- Half cup oat milk
- One teaspoon cumin

Directions:

Step 1

To begin, preheat the oven to 425° F.

Step 2

Place the parsnips in a medium bowl. Cover them uniformly with salt, oil, nutmeg, and pepper.

Step 3

Decrease the oven to 400°F. Toast parsnips for 20 minutes. Roast for an additional 10 minutes, or until the parsnips are soft.

Step 4

In a broad saucepan, melt butter over moderately low heat. Sauté for six minutes with leeks, celery, and onions.

Step 5

Combine the pears, parsnips, vegetable broth, sugar, bay leaf, and one teaspoon of rosemary in a medium mixing bowl. Bring to a boil, covered over medium-high heat. Remove the lid and continue simmering for another 25 minutes.

Step 6

Strain broth, discarding the bay leaf. With an immersion blender, blend soup until smooth in a stand blender or with a hand blender. Blend for 30 seconds, adding oat milk.

Step 7

Arrange in bowls and garnish with three pear slices sprinkled with the remaining teaspoon of minced rosemary and ground cumin.

Nutrition Facts:

Per Serving:
✓ Fat 10 g

- ✓ Calories 244
- ✓ Cholesterol 15 mg
- ✓ Sugar 19 g
- ✓ Carbohydrate 39 g
- ✓ Fiber 7 g
- ✓ Sodium 136 mg
- ✓ Protein 3 g
- ✓ Calcium 96 mg
- ✓ Potassium 497 mg
- ✓ Phosphorus 101 mg

Red Lentil Soup

Total Time: 35 minutes

Servings: 4

Difficulty level:

Ingredients:

- One cup red lentils (rinsed)
- Four cups water
- One small red beet, cut into 1-inch cubes
- Two teaspoons ground coriander
- Half teaspoon ground cumin
- Half teaspoon turmeric
- One large bay leaf
- Two small green Thai chili, or *jalapeño*
- Three tablespoons olive oil

- One-Fourth teaspoon black pepper
- Four sprigs cilantro
- One lemon

Directions:

Step 1

In a heavy three-quart pan, add the red lentils and 4 cups of water.

Step 2

Bring to a full boil over high heat. Occasionally, stir.

Step 3

Ensure that any foam that floats on top is removed.

Step 4

Combine the beets, bay leaf, spices, Thai chile or jalapeo pepper, and olive oil in a medium bowl.

Step 5

Combine thoroughly and bring mixture back to a boil. Reduce to a medium-low heat and cover tightly with a lid.

Step 6

Simmer for about 20 minutes, or until the beets and lentils are tender and cooked through.

Step 7

Turn the heat down. Leave the lid off the pot to enable the soup to cool.

Step 8

Discard the bay leaf and season with salt and pepper, if using.

Step 9

Using an immersion blender, puree the soup to the right consistency. If you want a thinner consistency, add additional water.

Step 10

Garnish with cilantro and lime juice and serve.

Nutrition Facts:

Per Serving:
✓ Calories 281
✓ Cholesterol 0 mg
✓ Fat 11 g
✓ Carbohydrate 35 g
✓ Protein 12 g
✓ Fiber 6 g
✓ Sodium 17 mg
✓ Phosphorus 162 mg
✓ Calcium 41 mg
✓ Potassium 462 mg

Kidney Bean and Vegetable Soup

Total Time: 1 hour

Servings: 4

Difficulty level: low

Ingredients:

- One tablespoon olive oil
- Salt to taste
- One chopped yellow onion
- Two chopped carrots
- One minced garlic clove

- Two teaspoons sodium-free chili powder
- Four cups low-fat chicken broth (low-sodium)
- One teaspoon ground cumin
- Two (15 oz.) cans kidney beans (low-sodium)
- One-Fourth teaspoon fresh ground black pepper
- One cup frozen whole kernel corn
- One (14.5 oz.) can stewed tomatoes (low-sodium)

Directions:

Step 1

In a large saucepan over medium heat, warm the olive oil.

Step 2

Cook, stirring occasionally, until the minced garlic, yellow onion, and carrots are tender.

Step 3

Add the ground cumin and chilli powder and cook for 60 seconds, stirring continuously.

Step 4

Put to a boil the chicken broth, frozen whole kernel corn, one can of kidney beans, and freshly ground black pepper.

Step 5

While the soup is heating, puree the second can of kidney beans and stewed tomatoes in a food processor until smooth; then incorporate into the soup.

Step 6

Season with salt to taste.

Step 7

Reduce to a low heat, cover, and cook for approximately 15 minutes.

Step 8

Allow to cool slightly before serving.

Nutrition Facts:

Per Serving:
- ✓ Calories 399.4
- ✓ Cholesterol 0 mg
- ✓ Fat 5.3 g
- ✓ Potassium 400 mg
- ✓ Sodium 30 mg
- ✓ Fiber 19.1 g
- ✓ Carbohydrate 71.7 g
- ✓ Protein 21.7 g
- ✓ Phosphorus 120 mg

Navy Bean Stew

Total Time: 6-8 hours

Servings: 6

Difficulty level: low

Ingredients:

- One lb. navy beans
- Two cans (15 ounces each) tomatoes (no salt added)
- One chopped onion
- One cup grated carrots
- Two tablespoons pepper

- Half tablespoon taste of Louisiana
- Three garlic cloves
- Two cups bouillon chicken (sodium free)

Directions:

Step 1

Soak one pound of navy beans overnight according to package instructions.

Step 2

Combine with the residual water in the slow cooker.

Step 3

Combine the tomato sauce, taste of Louisiana rub, shredded carrots, onion, black pepper, garlic, and chicken broth in a large mixing bowl.

Step 4

Combine thoroughly and cook over low heat for six-eight hours.

Step 5

Serve directly after portioning one cup into a serving dish.

Step 6

Keep leftovers refrigerated for up to three days.

Nutrition Facts:

Per Serving:
- ✓ Calories 264.21
- ✓ Carbohydrates 48.95 g
- ✓ Fat 1.27 g
- ✓ Protein 16.78 g

- ✓ Sodium 23.44 mg
- ✓ Fiber 18.98 g
- ✓ Phosphorus 100 mg
- ✓ Potassium 390 mg
- ✓ Cholesterol 0 mg

Barley & Vegetable Soup

Total Time: 30 minutes

Servings: 6

Difficulty level: low

Ingredients:

- Three-Fourth cup pearl barley
- Salt to taste
- Two tablespoons extra-virgin olive oil
- Eleven cups vegetable stock
- One and a half cups chopped onion
- Half cup chopped celery
- One cup chopped carrots
- One cup thinly sliced mushrooms
- Half bunch parsley

Directions:

Step 1

Mix the barley and three cups of vegetable stock in a saucepan.

Step 2

Bring to a simmer over medium heat, reduce to a low flame, lid, and boil for one hour, or until the fluid has been absorbed.

Step 3

In the meantime, in a large saucepan, heat the olive oil and include the onion, celery, carrots, and mushrooms.

Step 4

Cook, covered, for approximately 5 minutes, or until the vegetables begin to soften.

Step 5

Add the rest of the vegetable stock and cook, covered, for 30 minutes.

Step 6

Stir in the barley and cook for an additional 5 minutes.

Step 7

Season to taste with salt and spoon into bowls.

Step 8

Garnish with fresh parsley, if desired.

Nutrition Facts:

Per Serving:
- Calories 202.6
- Fat 5.1 g
- Protein 6.6 g
- Carbohydrate 33.7 g
- Cholesterol 0.0 mg
- Fiber 4.6 g

- ✓ Calcium 36.7 mg
- ✓ Potassium 462 mg
- ✓ Sodium 14 mg
- ✓ Phosphorus 162 mg

Chapter 7: Snacks

Egg Muffs

Total Time: 40 minutes

Servings: 8

Difficulty level: low

Ingredients:

- One cup onion
- One cup red, orange and yellow bell peppers
- Half pound ground pork
- One-Fourth teaspoon poultry seasoning
- One-Fourth teaspoon garlic powder
- Half teaspoon blend herb seasoning
- One-Fourth teaspoon onion powder
- Eight large eggs
- Pinch of salt

- Two tablespoons milk

Directions:

Step 1

Spray a standard size muffin tin with cooking spray and preheat the oven to 350° F.

Step 2

Finely chop the onion and bell peppers.

Step 3

To make the sausage, mix together pork, onion powder, garlic powder, poultry seasoning, and herb seasoning in a mixing bowl.

Step 4

Cook sausage crumbles until finished in a non-stick skillet; rinse.

Step 5

Mix the milk, eggs, and salt together in a mixing bowl.

Step 6

Stir in the sausage crumbles and vegetables.

Step 7

Pour the egg mixture into the muffin tins, leaving enough space for the muffins to grow. Preheat the oven to 180° F and bake for eighteen to twenty-two minutes.

Nutrition Facts:

Per Serving:
- ✓ Calories 154
- ✓ Sodium 155 mg
- ✓ Protein 12 g
- ✓ Fat 10 g

- ✓ Potassium 200 mg
- ✓ Carbohydrates 3 g
- ✓ Fiber 0.5 g
- ✓ Cholesterol 230 mg
- ✓ Phosphorus 154 mg
- ✓ Calcium 37 mg

Turkey In Buns

Total Time: 30 minutes

Servings: 6

Difficulty level: low

Ingredients:

- Half cup green bell pepper
- Half cup red onion
- One and a half pounds ground turkey, 7% fat
- Two tablespoons brown sugar
- One tablespoon chicken grilling blend seasoning
- One tablespoon Worcestershire sauce
- Six hamburger buns
- One cup low-sodium tomato sauce

Directions:

Step 1

Chop the bell pepper and onion into small pieces.

Step 2

Combine all ingredients in a large skillet with the turkey, and cook over medium-high heat until the turkey is fully cooked. Draining is not recommended.

Step 3

Combine the sugar, spice, tomato and Worcestershire sauce in a small bowl.

Step 4

Season the turkey mixture with seasonings. Cook for ten minutes on a low heat.

Step 5

Serve on hamburger buns, divided into six parts.

Nutrition Facts:

Per Serving:
- Calories 290
- Sodium 288 mg
- Protein 24 g
- Cholesterol 58 mg
- Potassium 513 mg
- Fat 9 g
- Carbohydrates 28 g
- Fiber 1.8 g
- Phosphorus 237 mg
- Calcium 86 mg

Maple And Honey Trail Mix

Total Time: 35 minutes

Servings: 24

Difficulty level: low

Ingredients:

- Three oz. Crispy Apple Chips
- Three cups Grahams cereal
- Ten oz. Cinnamon snack cookies
- Five cups Rice Chex cereal
- Six oz. Pretzel Crisps
- One-Third cup dark brown sugar
- Half cup unsalted butter
- One-Fourth cup maple syrup
- One-Fourth cup honey
- Five oz. dried and sweetened cranberries

Directions:

Step 1

In a big mixing bowl, combine the rice chex, grahams cereal, pretzels and cinnamon cookies.

Step 2

In a small saucepan, melt the butter; add honey, maple syrup and brown sugar. Cook, stirring constantly, until the sugar has melted.

Step 3

Pour over the cereal mixture and toss well to coat all the pieces thoroughly.

Step 4

Preheat the oven to 325° F.

Step 5

Line three jelly roll pans with aluminum foil that has been sprayed with cooking spray. (This can be achieved in three batches.) Using a spatula, uniformly distribute the cereal mixture between the pans. Keep the oven at 325°F and bake for twenty minutes, stirring halfway through.

Step 6

Combine apple chips and cranberries in a mixing bowl; split evenly between pans and stir.

Step 7

Bake for an additional 5 minutes, then cool fully before storing in an airtight jar.

Nutrition Facts:

Per Serving:
✓ Calories 262
✓ Sodium 178 mg
✓ Protein 3 g
✓ Cholesterol 11 mg
✓ Fat 9 g
✓ Potassium 84 mg
✓ Carbohydrates 47 g
✓ Fiber 1.8 g
✓ Phosphorus 66 mg
✓ Calcium 63 mg

Heavenly Challah

Total Time: 3 hours

Servings: 32

Difficulty level: low

Ingredients:

- Two tablespoons dry baker's yeast
- Seven cups all-purpose flour
- One large egg
- Six tablespoons sugar
- Half cup vegetable oil
- Two and a half cups warm water
- Two teaspoons salt

Directions:

Step 1

In a big mixing bowl, combine the yeast, flour, sugar, oil and water. Make the dough by kneading it. When you've shaped a ball, add the salt. Place the dough on a lightly floured sheet or surface and knead it for another ten minutes, or until it is smooth, soft, and not sticky.

Step 2

Use one to two teaspoons of oil to coat the bowl and dough. Plastic wrap the bowl and keep it warm until the dough has doubled in size. It should take one to two hours.

Step 3

Knead the dough for several minutes after it has risen. Cut the dough into twelve parts and roll each one into a braiding strand that is around ten to twelve inches long.

Step 4

To make the challah, braid three of the prepared dough strips together. To make four challahs, repeat with the remaining dough strips.

Step 5

Arrange the challahs in a baking tray, cover, and let rise for another 40 minutes.

Step 6

Preheat the oven to 350° F. Every challah should be brushed with beaten egg. Then bake the challahs for half hour, or until golden brown. Remove the challahs from the oven and place them on a wire rack to cool. Serve.

Nutrition Facts:

Per Serving:
- ✓ Calories 144
- ✓ Sodium 149 mg
- ✓ Protein 3 g
- ✓ Cholesterol 6 mg
- ✓ Fat 4 g
- ✓ Potassium 39 mg
- ✓ Carbohydrates 24 g
- ✓ Fiber 0.9 g
- ✓ Phosphorus 37 mg
- ✓ Calcium 6 mg

Spicy Turkey Barbecue Wings

Total Time: 1 hour 15 minutes

Servings: 7

Difficulty level: low

Ingredients:

- Barbecue Spice Rub
- One teaspoon black pepper
- Seven whole turkey wings
- One cup packed dark brown sugar
- One teaspoon red pepper flakes
- Two teaspoons granulated garlic
- One teaspoon smoked paprika
- Two teaspoons dark chili powder
- Two teaspoons dehydrated onion flakes
- Fourteen tablespoons any low-sodium barbecue sauce

Directions:

Step 1

Preheat the oven to 375° F.

Step 2

Dry the wings and pierce both sides with a fork.

Step 3

Liberally coat wings in the spice rub, reserving one tablespoon for later.

Step 4

Arrange wings on a baking tray and bake for half hour, covered in foil. Remove the wings from the oven, discard the foil, and cook for another half hour. Return the wings to their original location and season with the remaining seasoning.

Step 5

Remove wings from oven and set aside for 15 minutes. Before serving, add a barbecue sauce on the side which is low in sodium.

Nutrition Facts:

Per Serving:
- ✓ Calories 272
- ✓ Sodium 371 mg
- ✓ Protein 19 g
- ✓ Cholesterol 48 mg
- ✓ Fat 2 g
- ✓ Potassium 321 mg
- ✓ Carbohydrates 46 g
- ✓ Fiber 0.6 g
- ✓ Phosphorus 155 mg
- ✓ Calcium 54 mg

Cinnamon and Orange Biscotti

Total Time: 1 hour 10 minutes

Servings: 18

Difficulty level: low

Ingredients:

- One cup sugar
- One-Fourth teaspoon salt
- Two large eggs
- Two cups all-purpose flour
- Half teaspoon baking soda
- Half cup unsalted butter
- Two teaspoons grated orange peel
- One teaspoon vanilla extract
- One teaspoon cream of tartar
- One teaspoon ground cinnamon

Directions:

Step 1

Preheat the oven to 325° F (180° degrees Celsius).

Step 2

Lightly brush two baking sheets with non-stick cooking spray.

Step 3

In a big mixing bowl, mix together the unsalted butter, sugar and cream until smooth.

Step 4

Add the eggs one at a time, beating thoroughly after each addition.

Step 5

Add the vanilla extract and orange peel, and beat until combined.

Step 6

In a medium-sized mixing bowl, whisk together the salt, flour, cinnamon, baking soda, and cream of tartar.

Step 7

Stir in the dry ingredients until they are fully absorbed into the butter mixture.

Step 8

Separate the dough into two equal parts. Place one half on top of the other on a baking sheet that has been prepared. Shape each half into a wide three-inch, three-quarter-inch-high log shape with lightly floured hands. Bake for 35 minutes, or until the dough logs are firm to the touch.

Step 9

Take the dough logs out of the oven and set them aside for 10 minutes to cool.

Step 10

Lay the logs out on the work surface. Cut on the diagonal with a serrated knife into thick half-inch slices. Place on baking sheets with cut side down.

Step 11

Bake for around 12 minutes, or until the bottoms are golden.

Step 12

Turn biscotti over and bake for another 12 minutes or until bottoms are golden.

Step 13

Cool fully on a wire rack then serve.

Nutrition Facts:

Per Serving:
- ✓ Calories 149 cal
- ✓ Sodium 76 mg
- ✓ Protein 2 g
- ✓ Cholesterol 34 mg
- ✓ Fat 6 g
- ✓ Potassium 53 mg
- ✓ Fiber 0.5 g
- ✓ Phosphorus 28 mg
- ✓ Calcium 9 mg
- ✓ Carbohydrates 22 g

Buffalo Chicken Salad Stuffed In Cucumber Cups

Total Time: 20 minutes

Servings: 8

Difficulty level: low

Ingredients:

- Two large, shallow, seedless cucumbers sliced into 1-inch pieces
- Half teaspoon Italian seasoning
- One-Fourth cup blue cheese crumbs
- One tablespoon chopped fresh garlic
- Half teaspoon black pepper
- One teaspoon cayenne pepper
- Two tablespoons hot sauce

- Half cup mayonnaise
- Three cups shredded chicken breast
- Two tablespoons lemon juice
- Two tablespoons chopped fresh chives
- One teaspoon smoked paprika
- One-Fourth cup chopped fresh parsley

Directions:

Step 1

In a medium-sized mixing bowl, mix all the ingredients excluding the cucumbers and chicken.

Step 2

Add the chicken in the mixture and toss to cover evenly. Set aside for thirty minutes in the refrigerator.

Step 3

Take the cucumber slices out of the refrigerator and scoop equal quantities into each one. Serve with chopped parsley as a garnish.

Nutrition Facts:

Per Serving:
- ✓ Calories 155 cal
- ✓ Sodium 252 mg
- ✓ Protein 18 g
- ✓ Cholesterol 53 mg
- ✓ Fat 13 g
- ✓ Potassium 283 mg

- ✓ Carbohydrates 4 g
- ✓ Fiber 0.6 g
- ✓ Phosphorus 159 mg
- ✓ Calcium 47 mg

Herbed Biscuits

Total Time: 10 minutes

Servings: 12

Difficulty level: low

Ingredients:

- Three tablespoons any herb, dry or fresh
- Half teaspoon baking soda
- One teaspoon cream of tartar
- One-Fourth cup mayonnaise
- Non-stick cooking spray
- Two-Third cup skim milk
- One and a half cups of all-purpose flour

Directions:

Step 1

Preheat the oven to 400° F (200° degrees Celsius). Spray a baking tray with non-stick cooking spray after that.

Step 2

Combine the baking soda, rice and cream of tartar in a large mixing bowl. Then, using a fork, stir in the mayonnaise.

Step 3

Combine the herbs and milk in a small bowl and stir into the flour mixture. Stir until everything is well blended.

Step 4

Spoon generous tablespoons of the mixture onto the cookie sheet and place it for ten minutes in the oven.

Step 5

Once ready, store in the refrigerator.

Nutrition Facts:

Per Serving:
- ✓ Calories 109 cal
- ✓ Sodium 88 mg
- ✓ Protein 3 g
- ✓ Cholesterol 2 mg
- ✓ Fat 4 g
- ✓ Potassium 85 mg
- ✓ Carbohydrates 15 g
- ✓ Fiber 1 g
- ✓ Phosphorus 34 mg
- ✓ Calcium 21 mg

Yummy Protein Bars

Total Time: 1 hour 10 minutes

Servings: 12

Difficulty level: low

Ingredients:

- One cup blueberries or dried cherries
- Half cup peanut butter
- Two and a half cups toasted rolled oats
- Half cup flaxseeds
- Half cup honey
- Half cup almonds

Directions:

Step 1

To toast the oats, place on a baking sheet and toast until golden brown in a 350° F oven.

Step 2

Add all the ingredients in a large mixing bowl and stir until fully combined.

Step 3

Press the protein mixture into a 9 x 9 inch baking pan that has been lightly greased. Wrap in plastic wrap and chill for at least one hour, preferably overnight.

Step 4

To serve, break the protein bars into preferred squares.

Nutrition Facts:

Per Serving:
- ✓ Calories 283
- ✓ Sodium 49 mg
- ✓ Protein 7 g
- ✓ Cholesterol 0 mg
- ✓ Fat 13 g
- ✓ Potassium 258 mg
- ✓ Carbohydrates 39 g
- ✓ Fiber 5.8 g
- ✓ Phosphorus 177 mg
- ✓ Calcium 51 mg

Almond Pecan Caramel Corn

Total Time: 1 hour

Servings: 10

Difficulty level: low

Ingredients:

- One teaspoon baking soda
- One cup pecan halves
- Three-Fourth cup popcorn kernels or twenty cups popped popcorn
- One cup granulated sugar
- Two cups unblanched almonds
- Half cup corn syrup

- One cup unsalted butter
- A pinch of cream of tartar

Directions:

Step 1

Evenly layer cooked popcorn with almonds and pecans in a large roasting pan.

Step 2

Mix the cream of tartar, sugar, corn syrup, and butter together in a big heavy saucepan.

Step 3

Bring to a boil, stirring continuously, over medium-high heat. Enable to boil for five minutes, stirring periodically.

Step 4

Take the pan off the heat and whisk in the baking soda.

Step 5

Pour the caramel uniformly over the popcorn mixture and swirl to completely coat it.

Step 6

Bake for one hour at 200 degrees, stirring for every ten minutes.

Step 7

Allow to cool fully, stirring periodically. For up to one week, store in an airtight tin.

Nutrition Facts:

Per Serving:
- ✓ Calories 604
- ✓ Sodium 149 mg
- ✓ Protein 8 g
- ✓ Cholesterol 11 mg

- ✓ Fat 6 g
- ✓ Potassium 285 mg
- ✓ Carbohydrates 51 g
- ✓ Fiber 4 g
- ✓ Phosphorus 201 mg
- ✓ Calcium 73 mg

Quiche

Total Time: 1 hour 5 minutes

Servings: 6

Difficulty level: low

Ingredients:

- Four oz. grated cheese
- Two cups total filling
- Six eggs
- One 9-inch deep-dish frozen pie shell
- One cup 2% or lower milk

Directions:

Step 1

Preheat the oven to 350° F (180° degrees Celsius).

Step 2

Combine the milk, cheese, filling, and eggs in a mixing dish. If your phosphorus is elevated use two oz. of cheese.

Step 3

Pour into a frozen pie shell.

Step 4

Bake for 45 to 60 minutes in the oven, or until a knife inserted in the middle comes out clean.

Step 5

Cool for five minutes and serve.

(Remaining meat or vegetables, such as chicken, mushrooms, asparagus, or onions, may be used as a filling.)

Nutrition Facts:

Per Serving:
- ✓ Calories 356
- ✓ Sodium 409 mg
- ✓ Protein 16 g
- ✓ Cholesterol 11 mg
- ✓ Fat 9g
- ✓ Potassium 257 mg
- ✓ Carbohydrates 24 g
- ✓ Phosphorus 278 mg
- ✓ Calcium 54 mg
- ✓ Fiber 22 g

Mix Snacks

Total Time: 1 hour 15 minutes

Servings: 24

Difficulty level:

Ingredients:

- Three cups Cheerios
- One cup Kix
- Three cups Crispix
- Three cups Corn Flakes
- One cup Pretzels
- One cup broken Bagel Chips
- Two tablespoons Worcestershire sauce
- Three-Fourth teaspoon garlic powder
- Half teaspoon onion powder
- Six tablespoons margarine
- One and a half teaspoons seasoning salt

Directions:

Step 1

Preheat the oven to 250° F.

Step 2

In a big roasting pan, melt the margarine in the oven. Seasonings should be mixed in. Stir in the remaining ingredients in a slow, steady motion until they are uniformly distributed.

Step 3

Bake for one hour and fifteen minutes at a time, stirring halfway through. To cool, spread out on paper towels. You can store it in an airtight container to keep it fresh.

Nutrition Facts:

Per Serving:

- ✓ Calories: 88 Kcal
- ✓ Sodium: 190 mg
- ✓ Protein: 1.4 g
- ✓ Cholesterol 11 mg
- ✓ Fat: 3.4 g
- ✓ Potassium: 43.6 mg
- ✓ Carbohydrates: 13.7 g
- ✓ Fiber: 0.89 g
- ✓ Phosphorus: 25.1 mg
- ✓ Calcium 63 mg

Chapter 8: Salads

Goat Cheese and Strawberry Spring Salad

Total Time: 10 minutes

Servings: 4

Difficulty level: low

Ingredients:

- Five cups mixed baby lettuce
- One-Fourth teaspoon ground black pepper
- One pint fresh strawberries
- Two tablespoons balsamic vinegar
- Eight oz. soft goat cheese
- Three tablespoons extra virgin olive oil

Directions:

Step 1

Rinse and dry the lettuce; slice the strawberries vertically after removing the stems; divide the goat cheese into eight even sections.

Step 2

In a small cup, whisk together the olive oil and balsamic vinegar.

Step 3

Using a potato masher or fork, mash half of the strawberries together and add them to the dish. The consistency of the mixture should be chunky. Set aside the dressing mixture.

Step 4

In a wide bowl, position the lettuce. Combine the dressing, and season with salt and pepper to taste.

Step 5

Distribute the lettuce evenly across four plates. Cut the leftover strawberries and distribute them evenly among the salad plates. Each plate should be topped with two slices of goat cheese.

Step 6

Season with black pepper. Enjoy!

Nutrition Facts:

Per Serving:
- ✓ Calories 300
- ✓ Carbohydrates 11 g
- ✓ Protein 13 g
- ✓ Fat 23 g
- ✓ Sodium 289 mg
- ✓ Cholesterol 26 mg
- ✓ Potassium 404 mg
- ✓ Calcium 148 mg

- ✓ Phosphorus 195 mg
- ✓ Fiber 3.0 g

Summer Salad

Total Time: 5 minutes

Servings: 4

Difficulty level: low

Ingredients:

- One medium tomato
- One medium carrot
- Three cups iceberg lettuce
- One-Fourth medium cucumber

Directions:

Step 1

Cut the tomato and cucumber into slices; shred the carrot and lettuce.

Step 2

Toss vegetables in a bowl.

Step 3

Divide the salad into four equal amounts, and serve in salad bowls with a low-sodium dressing.

Nutrition Facts:

Per Serving:
- ✓ Calories 24
- ✓ Carbohydrates 5g

- ✓ Protein 1 g
- ✓ Fat 0 g
- ✓ Sodium 17 mg
- ✓ Cholesterol 0 mg
- ✓ Potassium 224 mg
- ✓ Calcium 22 mg
- ✓ Phosphorus 24 mg
- ✓ Fiber 1.6 g

Cucumber Salad

Total Time: 15 minutes

Servings: 1

Difficulty level: low

Ingredients:

- Four medium sliced cucumbers
- One medium sliced onion
- Half cup sugar
- One cup white vinegar
- Half cup water
- One-Fourth teaspoon salt
- Dill

Directions:

Step 1

In a cup, combine the onions and cucumbers. If using, season with salt and garnish with a sprig of dill.

Step 2

Bring vinegar, sugar, and water to a boil over medium-high heat, stirring constantly, until the sugar dissolves.

Step 3

Pour the vinegar mixture over cucumbers and toss well (while still hot). Allow at least thirty minutes to sit before serving. Refrigerate for 3-5 days.

Nutrition Facts:

Per Serving:
- ✓ Calories 28
- ✓ Cholesterol 0mg
- ✓ Fat 0.2g
- ✓ Potassium 191.8mg
- ✓ Sodium 77.3mg
- ✓ Fiber 1.1g
- ✓ Carbohydrate 4.6g
- ✓ Protein 0.8g
- ✓ Phosphorus 30mg

Kidney Bean Salad With Dijon Vinaigrette

Total Time: 15 minutes

Servings: 4

Difficulty level: low

Ingredients:

- One 15 ounces can kidney beans
- One medium-sized chopped tomato

- Half chopped cucumber
- One red chopped onion
- One bunch chopped fresh cilantro

Dijon Vinaigrette

- Salt and pepper
- One large lemon
- One teaspoon sumac
- One teaspoon Dijon mustard
- Threetablespoons extra virgin olive oil
- Half teaspoon fresh garlic paste, or finely chopped garlic

Directions:

Step 1

Mix the kidney beans, sliced vegetables, and cilantro in a medium-sized dish.

Step 2

To prepare the vinaigrette, whisk together the oil, lime juice, mustard, fresh garlic, sumac, and pepper in a separate small cup.

Step 3

Drizzle the vinaigrette over the salad and toss with a wide spoon until well combined. If necessary, season with salt and pepper.

Step 4

Cover and chill for 30 to 60 minutes before serving.

Nutrition Facts:

Per Serving:
- ✓ Calories 154

- ✓ Carbohydrate 18.3 g
- ✓ Fat 7.4g
- ✓ Protein 5.5g
- ✓ Phosphorus 32 mg
- ✓ Potassium 120 mg
- ✓ Calcium 34 mg
- ✓ Sodium 77.3mg
- ✓ Cholesterol 0mg
- ✓ Fiber 1.1g

Apple and Chicken Salad

Total Time: 10 minutes

Servings: 4

Difficulty level: low

Ingredients:

- Two cups cooked chicken
- One-Fourth teaspoon black pepper
- One-Fourth teaspoon cinnamon
- One cup gala apple
- Two tablespoons scallions
- Half cup celery
- One-Fourth cup dark raisins
- One tablespoon sour cream (low-fat)
- One-Third cup mayonnaise (low-fat)

- One teaspoon lemon juice

Directions:

Step 1

Cut the cooked chicken in cubes. Celery and apple should also be diced. Scallions should be chopped.

Step 2

In a big salad bowl, combine the apple, scallions, chicken, celery, and raisins.

Step 3

In a medium mixing bowl, combine the mayonnaise, lemon juice, sour cream, cinnamon, and black pepper. Toss in the chicken-apple mixture.

Step 4

Chill in the refrigerator prior to serving.

Nutrition Facts:

Per Serving:
- ✓ Calories 244
- ✓ Fiber 1.5 g
- ✓ Protein 21 g
- ✓ Fat 12 g
- ✓ Carbohydrates 13 g
- ✓ Calcium 32 mg
- ✓ Cholesterol 64 mg
- ✓ Potassium 350 mg
- ✓ Sodium 221 mg
- ✓ Phosphorus 158 mg

Chicken and Lemon Curry Salad

Total Time: 10 minutes

Servings: 4

Difficulty level: low

Ingredients:

- One-Eighth teaspoon garlic powder
- Four tablespoons frozen lemonade concentrate
- One and a half cups seedless green grapes
- One and a half cups cooked chicken breast
- Half cup celery
- One-Fourth teaspoon ground ginger
- One-Fourth cup canola oil
- One-Fourth teaspoon curry powder

Directions:

Step 1

Defrost the lemonade concentrate. Chicken should be diced. Grapes should be cut in half, and celery should be sliced.

Step 2

Combine the lemonade concentrate, oil, and spices in a big mixing bowl.

Step 3

Gently toss in remaining ingredients.

Step 4

Refrigerate before serving.

Nutrition Facts:

Per Serving:

- ✓ Calories 308
- ✓ Carbohydrates 15 g
- ✓ Protein 17 g
- ✓ Fat 20 g
- ✓ Sodium 57 mg
- ✓ Cholesterol 36 mg
- ✓ Potassium 235 mg
- ✓ Calcium 46 mg
- ✓ Phosphorus 119 mg
- ✓ Fiber 0.9 g

Colorful Garden Salad

Total Time: 30 minutes

Servings: 2

Difficulty level: low

Ingredients:

- One stalk celery
- One and a half cups Romaine lettuce
- Half diced small tomato
- Two cups iceberg lettuce
- Four shredded baby carrots
- Half red diced onion

- Half sliced cucumber

Directions:

Step 1

In a big mixing bowl, combine all the vegetables.

Step 2

To make the dressing, whisk together vinegar and oil, or use your favorite low sodium salad dressing. Have fun!

Nutrition Facts:

Per Serving:
- ✓ Calories 24
- ✓ Phosphorus 31.4 mg
- ✓ Carbohydrates 5.4 g
- ✓ Protein 1.1 g
- ✓ Fiber 1.8 g
- ✓ Fat 0.2 g
- ✓ Potassium 232.8 mg
- ✓ Sodium 18.6 mg
- ✓ Calcium 27.4 mg

Chicken Fruit Salad

Total Time: 10 minutes

Servings: 8

Difficulty level: low

Ingredients:

- Eight oz. small shell pasta, uncooked
- Three-Fourth cup mayonnaise
- Three cups cooked chicken
- One and a half cups seedless grapes
- One and a half cups celery
- Fifteen oz. canned mandarin oranges

Directions:

Step 1

Cut the cooked chicken in chunks. Celery should be sliced and grapes should be halved. Mandarin oranges should be drained.

Step 2

Prepare pasta according to the package directions, omitting the salt. Drain thoroughly and cool by rinsing in cold water.

Step 3

Add cooked pasta and the remaining ingredients in a big mixing bowl. Combine thoroughly.

Step 4

Cover and chill until ready to serve.

Nutrition Facts:

Per Serving:

- ✓ Calories 380
- ✓ Carbohydrates 31 g
- ✓ Protein 17 g
- ✓ Fat 21 g
- ✓ Sodium 183 mg
- ✓ Cholesterol 47 mg
- ✓ Potassium 291 mg
- ✓ Calcium 23 mg
- ✓ Phosphorus 159 mg
- ✓ Fiber 1.7 g

Grilled Chicken Salad

Total Time: 15 minutes

Servings: 4

Difficulty level:

Ingredients:

- Three tablespoons olive oil
- Two teaspoons garlic herb seasoning blend
- Three tablespoons red wine vinegar
- Twelve medium strawberries
- One-Fourth teaspoon salt
- Six cups butter head lettuce
- Four boneless, skinless chicken breasts

- Half small red onion
- Eight plain breadsticks

Directions:

Step 1

Combine the vinegar, olive oil, seasoning, and salt to make the dressing.

Step 2

Place chicken in a zip-top bag and cover with two tablespoons of the dressing.

Step 3

Preheat a grill to a medium-high temperature.

Step 4

Grill chicken breasts for 8–10 minutes, or until juices run clear and the chicken is cooked completely. Turn off the heat and allow to cool for 5 minutes.

Step 5

Tear lettuce into bite-size pieces. Cut onion rings in half.

Step 6

On a tray, arrange the lettuce, onion rings, and strawberries.

Step 7

Using a sharp knife, cut each breast lengthwise and arrange on lettuce bed.

Step 8

Drizzle each salad with 1 tablespoon of the remaining dressing.

Step 9

Arrange two breadsticks on top of each salad.

Nutrition Facts:

Per Serving
- ✓ Calories 308
- ✓ Carbohydrates 14 g
- ✓ Protein 29 g
- ✓ Fat 15 g
- ✓ Sodium 278 mg
- ✓ Cholesterol 70 mg
- ✓ Potassium 534 mg
- ✓ Calcium 55 mg
- ✓ Phosphorus 249 mg
- ✓ Fiber 2.2 g

Pineapple Coleslaw

Total Time: 10 minutes

Servings: 4

Difficulty level: low

Ingredients:

- Two cups shredded cabbage
- Dash of pepper
- One-Fourth cup chopped onion
- One 8 ounce can crushed unsweetened pineapple
- One-Fourth cup Miracle Whip

Directions:

Step 1

Combine all the ingredients.

Step 2

Refrigerate for at least one hour prior to serving.

Nutrition Facts:

Per Serving:
- ✓ Calories 72
- ✓ Protein 1 g
- ✓ Sodium 137 mg
- ✓ Potassium 153 mg
- ✓ Calcium 22 mg
- ✓ Fat 3 g
- ✓ Carbohydrates 11 g
- ✓ Fiber 1 g
- ✓ Phosphorus 15 mg
- ✓ Cholesterol 2 mg

Italian Eggplant Salad

Total Time: 10 minutes

Servings: 4

Difficulty level: low

Ingredients:

- Three cups cubed eggplant
- Two tablespoons white wine vinegar
- One small chopped onion
- One chopped garlic clove
- One-Fourth teaspoon black pepper
- Half teaspoon oregano
- Three tablespoons olive oil
- One medium chopped tomato

Directions:

Step 1

In a saucepan of boiling water, add eggplant.

Step 2

Bring to a boil and then reduce to a low heat.

Step 3

Cover and cook for approximately 10 minutes, or until tender; drain.

Step 4

In a glass bowl, combine the eggplant and onion.

Step 5

Combine the garlic, vinegar, and pepper in a small bowl.

Step 6

Drizzle over the onion and eggplant and toss to coat.

Step 7

Just before serving, stir in oil.

Nutrition Facts:

Per Serving:
- ✓ Calories 69
- ✓ Protein 1 g
- ✓ Sodium 2 mg
- ✓ Phosphorus 15 mg
- ✓ Potassium 118 mg
- ✓ Calcium 10 mg
- ✓ Fat 5 g
- ✓ Carbohydrates 6 g
- ✓ Fiber 1 g
- ✓ Cholesterol 2 mg

Crunchy Chicken Salad

Total Time: 5 minutes

Servings: 6

Difficulty level: low

Ingredients:

- Two cups cooked chicken
- One large hard-boiled egg
- Two tablespoons onion

- One-Fourth cup celery
- One-Fourth cup reduced-fat mayonnaise
- One teaspoon fresh lemon juice
- Half teaspoon sugar
- One-Fourth teaspoon black pepper

Directions:

Step 1

Shred or dice the chicken. Chop the onion, egg, and celery into small pieces.

Step 2

In a big mixing bowl, combine all ingredients.

Step 3

Refrigerate overnight or for at least two hours prior to serving.

Nutrition Facts:

Per Serving:
- ✓ Calories 127
- ✓ Carbohydrates 2 g
- ✓ Protein 16 g
- ✓ Fat 6 g
- ✓ Sodium 95 mg
- ✓ Cholesterol 75 mg
- ✓ Potassium 136 mg
- ✓ Calcium 14 mg
- ✓ Phosphorus 122 mg
- ✓ Fiber 0.2 g

Cool Coconut Marshmallow Salad

Total Time: 10 minutes

Servings: 8

Difficulty level: low

Ingredients:

- One can 15 oz. drained fruit cocktail
- One package 8.8 oz. fruit flavored marshmallows
- Two cups sour cream
- One cup dried shredded coconut

Directions:

Step 1

In a mixing bowl, combine all ingredients.

Step 2

Transfer to a serving glass cup.

Step 3

Put it in the fridge an hour prior to serving if you want a creamy salad.

Step 4

Refrigerate molded salad overnight.

Nutrition Facts:

Per Serving

- ✓ Calories 317
- ✓ Protein 3 g
- ✓ Sodium 48 mg
- ✓ Potassium 185 mg

- ✓ Calcium 64 mg
- ✓ Fat 18 g
- ✓ Carbohydrates 40 g
- ✓ Fiber 3 g
- ✓ Phosphorus 74 mg
- ✓ Cholesterol 22 mg

Italian Chicken Salad

Total Time: 10 minutes

Servings: 4

Difficulty level: low

Ingredients:

- Half cup mayonnaise
- Two cups baby arugula
- One-Fourth cup lemon juice
- One-Eighth teaspoon cayenne pepper
- Six sprigs Italian flat-leaf parsley
- Four chicken breasts, cooked
- One-Fourth cup sweet onion
- One red or orange bell pepper
- Two cups grilled summer squash

Directions:

Step 1

Snip two sprigs of parsley into small bits. Chop the bell pepper and onion finely. Squash can be cut into half-moons after grilling.

Step 2

In a mixing bowl, combine the mayonnaise, snipped parsley, lemon juice, and cayenne pepper (optional).

Step 3

Cut the chicken breast into 1/2-inch cubes.

Step 4

Toss the mayonnaise with the cubed chicken, pepper, onion, and squash.

Step 5

Refrigerate for at least an hour to allow flavors to meld.

Step 6

Spoon half a cup of baby arugula over the top. Garnish with the remaining 4 sprigs of parsley.

Nutrition Facts:

Per Serving:
- ✓ Calories 421
- ✓ Carbohydrates 10 g
- ✓ Protein 30 g
- ✓ Fat 29 g
- ✓ Sodium 256 mg
- ✓ Cholesterol 80 mg

- ✓ Potassium 670 mg
- ✓ Calcium 66 mg
- ✓ Phosphorus 270 mg
- ✓ Fiber 2.2 g

Purple Salad

Total Time: 10 minutes

Servings: 12

Difficulty level: low

Ingredients:

- Three cups shredded cabbage
- Half teaspoon black pepper
- One cup shredded carrots
- One medium cucumber, sliced thin
- One cup chopped red onion
- One-Fourth cup vinegar
- Two tablespoons lemon juice
- One-Fourth cup oil
- Half cup sugar

Directions:

Step 1

Combine the vinegar, sugar, lemon juice, oil, and black pepper in a mixing bowl. Place aside.

Step 2

In a big mixing bowl, combine the shredded cabbage, carrots, red onion, and cucumber slices.

Step 3

Drizzle the salad with dressing.

Nutrition Facts:

Per Serving
- Calories 90
- Protein 1 g
- Sodium 11 mg
- Potassium 162 mg
- Fat 5 g
- Carbohydrates 13 g
- Calcium 20 mg
- Phosphorus 26 mg
- Cholesterol 0 mg
- Fiber 1 g

Chapter 9: Pasta

Cheesy Pasta with Meat Sauce

Total Time: 30 minutes

Servings: 6

Difficulty level: low

Ingredients:

- Half box large shaped pasta
- One pound ground beef
- Half cup diced onions
- One tablespoon onion flakes
- One and a half cups beef stock (no sodium)
- One tablespoon beef (no salt)
- One tablespoon tomato sauce, no salt added
- Three-Fourth cup shredded cheese
- Eight oz. softened cream cheese

- Half teaspoon reduced sodium Italian seasoning
- Half teaspoon ground black pepper
- Two tablespoons Worcestershire sauce

Directions:

Step 1

Prepare the pasta noodles as per the package instructions.

Step 2

In a big sauté pan, brown the ground beef, onions, and onion flakes.

Step 3

Drain and combine the stock, bouillon, and tomato sauce in a medium bowl.

Step 4

Bring to a low heat and cook, stirring occasionally. Turn off heat and stir in the cooked pasta, shredded cheese, softened cream cheese, and seasonings (Italian seasoning, Worcestershire sauce and black pepper). Slow cook the pasta mixture until the cheese is fully melted.

Nutrition Facts:

Per Serving:
- ✓ Calories 502
- ✓ Cholesterol 99 mg
- ✓ Fat 30 g
- ✓ Sodium 401 mg
- ✓ Protein 23 g
- ✓ Carbohydrates 35 g
- ✓ Phosphorus 278 mg

- ✓ Fiber 1.7 g
- ✓ Potassium 549 mg
- ✓ Calcium 107 mg

Pasta Primavera

Total Time: 20 minutes

Servings: 6

Difficulty level: low

Ingredients:

- Twelve oz. pasta, uncooked
- Twelve oz. frozen mixed vegetables
- Fourteen oz. low-sodium chicken broth
- Two tablespoons all-purpose white flour
- One-Fourth cup half & half creamer
- One-Fourth teaspoon garlic powder
- One-Fourth cup grated Parmesan cheese

Directions:

Step 1

In separate pots, cook the vegetables and pasta according to package instructions, omitting salt.

Step 2

In a stockpot over low heat, pour the low-sodium chicken broth.

Step 3

Gradually whisk flour into the broth, being careful not to form clumps.

Step 4

Remove from heat and whisk in the garlic powder and half and half.

Step 5

Simmer for 5–10 minutes on low heat, or until the mixture slightly thickens. While simmering, periodically stir.

Step 6

Stir in the cooked pasta and vegetables. Cook over medium heat until fully heated.

Step 7

Serve with a sprinkle of Parmesan cheese.

Nutrition Facts:

Per Serving:
- ✓ Calories 273
- ✓ Carbohydrates 48 g
- ✓ Protein 13 g
- ✓ Fat 3 g
- ✓ Sodium 115 mg
- ✓ Cholesterol 6 mg
- ✓ Potassium 251 mg
- ✓ Calcium 93 mg
- ✓ Phosphorus 154 mg
- ✓ Fiber 4.5 g

Pesto Pronto

Total Time: 10 minutes

Servings: 6

Difficulty level: low

Ingredients:

- Sixteen ounce white pasta
- One-Fourth cup Feta Cheese
- Two medium Zucchini, sliced into half moons
- One large red bell pepper, diced
- One medium yellow squash, sliced into half moons
- Half cup mushrooms, sliced fairly thick
- Two garlic cloves
- Two tablespoons Olive Oil
- Two-Third cup Pesto Sauce

Directions:

Step 1

Heat oven to 425° F.

Step 2

On an 18 by 13-inch baking dish, arrange the zucchini, bell pepper, squash, onion, and mushrooms. Drizzle olive oil over the vegetables and toss to coat evenly.

Step 3

Roast until vegetables are tender in a preheated oven. While the vegetables roast, cook the pasta according to the package directions and drain.

Step 4

Transfer drained pasta to a large mixing bowl. Toss in the roasted vegetables and pesto until evenly coated. Serve immediately.

Nutrition Facts:

Per Serving:
- ✓ Fat 18.8g
- ✓ Sodium 336.3mg
- ✓ Cholesterol 5.6mg
- ✓ Carbohydrate 66.9 g
- ✓ Protein 13.4g
- ✓ Fiber 4.3g
- ✓ Potassium 476mg
- ✓ Calories 492
- ✓ Phosphorus 237mg

Vegetable Pasta Salad

Total Time: 40

Servings: 8

Difficulty level: low

Ingredients:

- One tablespoon Garlic, minced
- One-Fourth cup Lemon juice
- One tablespoon Dijon mustard
- One-Fourth cup extra extra virgin olive oil

- Sixteen ounces pasta, uncooked
- One-Half teaspoon Black pepper
- One teaspoon Thyme
- Two medium Zucchinis, sliced
- One medium Red onion, sliced
- Eight White mushrooms, quartered
- Sixteen oz. Chicken breast
- Two tablespoons Basil
- One tablespoon Parsley

Directions:

Step 1

To make the dressing, whisk together the black pepper, lemon juice, Dijon mustard, olive oil, and garlic in a bowl and mix.

Step 2

In a separate big mixing bowl, combine all of the vegetables. Distribute half of the dressing on the vegetables and toss to cover lightly. Set aside vegetables.

Step 3

Prepare the pasta according to the package instructions. Rinse it under cold running water.

Step 4

Cut the chicken breast and add to the pan while the pasta is cooking. Cook until golden brown.

Step 5

In a sauté pan, sauté vegetables, or preheat oven to broil, and then spread the vegetables on a greased broiler pan.

Step 6

Cook vegetables until they are a golden brown colour. Stir every 4 to 5 mins if broiling until golden brown is reached.

Step 7

Pour into a large serving bowl and add the pasta, herbs, remaining dressing, and chicken. Serve immediately after tossing.

Step 8

If desired, chill pasta salad for 1 hour before serving.

Nutrition Facts:

Per Serving:
- ✓ Fat 11 g
- ✓ Carbohydrates 48 mg
- ✓ Fiber 4 g
- ✓ Protein 26 g
- ✓ Sodium 9 mg
- ✓ Calories 390
- ✓ Phosphorus 237mg
- ✓ Potassium 476mg
- ✓ Cholesterol 5.6mg

Creamy Lemon Salmon Pasta

Total Time: 30 minutes

Servings: 5

Difficulty level:

Ingredients:

- One can 14oz. salmon
- One box (16oz) pasta
- Half cup lemon juice
- Four cups broccoli, cooked
- One-Fourth onion, diced
- One tablespoon canola or olive oil
- Two cups unsweetened rice milk
- One-Fourth cup chopped fresh parsley
- One-Fourth cup corn starch

Directions:

Step 1

Salmon that has been canned should be drained and rinsed. After rinsing, drizzle 14 cups of lemon juice over canned salmon and allow to sit for 5-10 min.

Step 2

Cook the pasta as per package directions, drain, and rinse under cold running water.

Step 3

Broccoli, blanched (Blanch technique—Blanch broccoli for 2 minutes in boiling water, then remove and cool in ice water.)

Step 4

Heat oil in a large frying pan. Sauté onions until translucent, around 3-5 minutes.

Step 5

Bring 2 cups of milk to a boil in a saucepan. If a richer sauce is needed, increase the amount of milk in the pan to 12 cups and bring to a simmer. Combine the remaining 12 cups of rice milk and cornstarch in a slurry. When the liquid is heating, whisk the slurry into the skillet.

Step 6

Reduce to a simmer, add the salmon, and cook for an additional 2 minutes. Re-introduce the pasta and broccoli and get back to a simmer. Remove from heat and garnish with chopped parsley (optional).

Nutrition Facts:

Per Serving:
- ✓ Calories 350
- ✓ Potassium 540mg
- ✓ Sodium 250mg
- ✓ Carbohydrate 55g
- ✓ Phosphorus 40 mg
- ✓ Protein 20g
- ✓ Cholesterol 5.6mg
- ✓ Fat 11g
- ✓ Fiber 7 g
- ✓ Protein 26 g

Pasta With Kidney Bean Sauce

Total Time: 15 minutes

Servings: 2

Difficulty level: low

Ingredients:

- Seven oz. pasta of your choice
- Two cloves of garlic
- One onion
- One can of kidney beans
- Two tablespoons tomato paste
- Two tablespoons balsamic vinegar
- Dash of liquid smoke
- Half teaspoon cayenne pepper
- Half teaspoon smoked paprika
- One teaspoon dried oregano
- Salt and pepper
- Handful of arugula

Directions:

Step 1

Prepare the pasta as per the directions on the box.

Step 2

In a big pan with some tablespoons of water, dice the onion and mince the garlic. Cook for approximately 5 minutes, or until the liquid is translucent.

Step 3

Cook for an additional 5-10 minutes before adding the strained beans, tomato paste, balsamic vinegar, oregano, paprika, liquid smoke, cayenne pepper, and salt and pepper. If the mixture is too thick, add a little more water. If you want a smoother texture, lightly mash beans with a fork.

Step 4

Serve warm over pasta with arugula on top. Take pleasure!

Nutrition Facts:

Per Serving:
- ✓ Calories 144
- ✓ Fiber 2.8 g
- ✓ Carbohydrates 21.9 g
- ✓ Protein 5.9 g
- ✓ Sodium 55.1 mg
- ✓ Fat 4.3 g
- ✓ Potassium 355.2 mg
- ✓ Phosphorus 97.8 mg
- ✓ Calcium 51.3 mg

Cheese and Macaroni

Total Time: 20 minutes

Servings: 4

Difficulty level: low

Ingredients:

- Two cups macaroni
- Half cup grated cheddar cheese
- Three cups boiling water
- One-Fourth teaspoon dried mustard
- One teaspoon margarine or salt free butter

Directions:

Step 1

Bring water to a boil, add macaroni and cook for approximately 5-7 minutes, or until tender.

Step 2

Remove the water.

Step 3

Sprinkle with cheese and stir in mustard and butter while still very hot.

Step 4

Bake for 10 - 15 minutes at 350° degrees or until the top is nicely browned for an added crunch.

Nutrition Facts:

Per Serving:
- ✓ Calories 163

- ✓ Protein 6 g
- ✓ Sodium 114 mg
- ✓ Potassium 39 mg
- ✓ Calcium 120 mg
- ✓ Fat 7 g
- ✓ Carbohydrates 20 g
- ✓ Fiber 3 g
- ✓ Phosphorus 138 mg
- ✓ Cholesterol 17 mg

Baked Broccoli and Cauliflower Mac-n-Cheese

Total Time: 30 minutes

Servings: 8

Difficulty level: low

Ingredients:

- Twelve oz. penne pasta
- Two cups broccoli florets
- Two cups cauliflower florets
- Four tablespoons unsalted butter
- One garlic clove
- Half cup onion
- Three tablespoons all-purpose flour
- Half teaspoon black pepper
- Two and a half cups classic original rice drink
- One-Fourth teaspoon nutmeg

- One cup shredded sharp white cheddar cheese
- Two tablespoons spicy brown mustard
- One cup shredded Swiss cheese
- One cup panko-style bread crumbs
- Half cup shredded parmesan cheese

Directions:

Step 1

Heat oven to 350° F.

Step 2

Bring a saucepan of water to a boil. Add the pasta and cook for an additional 2 minutes.

Step 3

Steam cauliflower and broccoli florets for 5 minutes, or until tender in a separate covered pan. Discard and set aside. Eliminate liquid from the pot.

Step 4

Finely cut the garlic clove and onion.

Step 5

Melt three tablespoons of butter in the same pot over medium heat, then include the garlic and onion. Sauté for 4 minutes, or until the vegetables are tender. Whisk in flour for 1 minute. Sprinkle with pepper and nutmeg. Whisk in rice drink. Stir until smooth, then add the spicy mustard.

Step 6

Combine all three cheeses. Stir in 2/3 of the blended cheeses until melted.

Step 7

Rinse pasta. Stir in the cauliflower and broccoli, followed by the cheese sauce.

Step 8

Coat a 9" x 12" baking dish with non-stick cooking spray, and spoon the pasta mixture into the prepared pan. Finish with the remainder of the blended cheeses.

Step 9

Place baking pan on a baking tray in the oven to trap any overflowing liquid. Increase oven temperature to 400° F after 30 minutes of baking. Add the leftover 1 tablespoon butter and one cup of bread crumbs to sautéd 1 tablespoon butter and 1 cup bread crumbs to top of casserole. Cook for an additional 8–10 minutes, or until crumbs are golden brown.

Nutrition Facts:

Per Serving:
- ✓ Calories 442
- ✓ Carbohydrates 52 g
- ✓ Protein 18 g
- ✓ Fat 18 g
- ✓ Sodium 308 mg
- ✓ Cholesterol 50 mg
- ✓ Potassium 278 mg
- ✓ Calcium 318 mg
- ✓ Phosphorus 315 mg
- ✓ Fiber 2.2 g

Creamy Shells With Bacon and Peas

Total Time: 30 minutes

Servings: 4

Difficulty level: low

Ingredients:

- Two cups Frozen Peas
- Six slices Bacon
- Eight ounces pasta shells
- Freshly ground black pepper
- Two tablespoons butter
- One-Third cup Creme Fraiche
- Two tablespoons diced shallots
- Two teaspoons Lemon Zest
- Parmesan cheese

Directions:

Step 1

Microwave they peas until they're just soft. Any excess water should be drained.

Step 2

Bring to a boil a big stockpot of salted water. Cook the pasta according to the package instructions. (Important: When the pasta is almost finished cooking, drain and conserve 1/2 cup of the pasta water using a measuring cup. Some of this may be needed to thin the sauce.)

Step 3

Preheat a large skillet over moderate flame while the pasta is cooking. When heated, add bacon and sauté for 8 to 10 minutes, or until golden and crisp. Shift bacon to a plate lined with paper towels.

Step 4

Empty the pan with all but a light coating of bacon grease.

Step 5

Reduce the heat to low-medium under the pan.

Step 6

Add the shallots and butter and sauté for 2 to 3 minutes, or until the shallots are very tender.

Step 7

Add peas to the shallots and cook for 1 minute.

Step 8

Turn off heat and remove pan.

Step 9

Add the crème fraîche, lemon zest and pasta to pan and mix.

Step 10

Garnish pasta with cooked bacon, freshly ground black pepper, and a sprinkle of parmesan cheese.

Nutrition Facts:

Per Serving:
- ✓ Calories: 491
- ✓ Protein: 16g
- ✓ Carbohydrates: 55g

- ✓ Fat: 23g
- ✓ Sodium: 280mg
- ✓ Cholesterol: 48mg
- ✓ Potassium: 395mg
- ✓ Calcium: 37mg
- ✓ Fiber: 6g

Ranch Chicken Pasta

Total Time: 30 minutes

Servings: 8

Difficulty level:

Ingredients:

- Sixteen oz. penne pasta
- One tablespoon all-purpose white flour
- One tablespoon butter
- Two teaspoons dried parsley flakes
- One cup unenriched rice milk
- One teaspoon salt-free, lemon pepper seasoning
- Half teaspoon dried minced onion
- Half teaspoon garlic powder
- Half teaspoon dill weed
- One-Eighth teaspoon pepper
- One-Fourth teaspoon onion powder
- One cup reduced-fat sour cream
- Half cup reduced-fat shredded Mexican cheese blend

- Two cups cooked chicken breast
- One-Fourth cup shredded parmesan cheese

Directions:

Step 1

Prepare the pasta according to package directions, omitting salt; wash and set aside.

Step 2

Melt butter in a big saucepan or Dutch oven. Add the flour and whisk until smooth.

Step 3

Add the seasonings and rice milk gradually.

Step 4

Increase the heat to high and bring to a simmer. Heat and mix for 2 minutes, or until the mixture becomes thickened.

Step 5

Reduce heat to low and stir in sour cream until smooth.

Step 6

Stir in the chicken and pasta. Continue cooking until thoroughly heated.

Step 7

Switch off the pan. Add the Mexican cheese blend and stir until melted. Serve sprinkled with parmesan cheese.

Nutrition Facts:

Per Serving:
- ✓ Calories 237
- ✓ Carbohydrates 23g
- ✓ Protein 16 g

- ✓ Fat 9 g
- ✓ Sodium 150 mg
- ✓ Cholesterol 49 mg
- ✓ Potassium 184 mg
- ✓ Calcium 136 mg
- ✓ Phosphorus 204 mg
- ✓ Fiber 0.9 g

Creamy Sweet Potato Pasta Bake

Total Time: 1 hour

Servings: 6

Difficulty level: low

Ingredients:

For Pasta:

- One and a half lbs. Sweet Potatoes, roasted
- One onion, finely diced
- Twelve ounces Fusilli Pasta
- Four ounces Sharp Cheddar Cheese, shredded
- One tablespoon Extra Virgin Olive Oil
- One-Fourth cup plain Greek Yogurt
- Two large Carrots, finely diced
- One and a half cups Low Sodium Vegetable Broth

For Topping:

- Two ounces parmesan cheese, finely grated

- Extra virgin olive oil
- Ten fresh sage leaves

Directions:

Step 1

Grease a 9x13 baking sheet lightly. Preheat oven to 350° F.

Step 2

Scoop the cooked sweet potatoes into a bowl and mash gently until nearly smooth.

Step 3

Cook the noodles as per package directions, but remove them from the heat 2-3 minutes earlier than instructed. Don't overcook.

Step 4

In a broad skillet over medium-high heat, heat the olive oil. When the oil is shimmering, add the carrots and onions and sauté for around 6-8 minutes, or until very tender. Gently stir in the mashed sweet potato and vegetable broth until the mixture begins to boil. Switch off the heat and extract the pan from the heat. Combine the greek yogurt, sweet potato sauce, cooked pasta, and cheddar cheese in a big mixing bowl. Stir well to combine. Distribute the pasta evenly in the prepared baking pan.

Step 5

Sprinkle parmesan cheese on top of the pasta. Every fresh sage leaf should be dipped in olive oil and scattered over the cheese. Bake for 15-17 minutes, or until thoroughly heated. Broil for about 2-3 minutes, or until the sage leaves are crisp and the parmesan is golden. Serve right away.

Nutrition Facts:

Per Serving:
- ✓ Calories 230

- ✓ Carbohydrates 20 g
- ✓ Protein 15 g
- ✓ Fat 10 g
- ✓ Sodium 130 mg
- ✓ Cholesterol 43 mg
- ✓ Potassium 130 mg
- ✓ Calcium 126 mg
- ✓ Phosphorus 200 mg
- ✓ Fiber 1 g

Chicken Enchilada Pasta

Total Time: 30 minutes

Servings: 4

Difficulty level: low

Ingredients:

- Eight ounces pasta
- Two cloves chopped garlic
- One tablespoon cooking oil
- Two cups shredded cooked chicken
- One and a half cups frozen corn
- Half teaspoon ground cumin
- One 4 ounce can mild green chiles
- Half teaspoon Paprika
- One 10 ounce can Red Enchilada Sauce

- One and a half cup cheddar cheese
- One 15 ounce can Fire-Roasted Diced Tomatoes
- Sour cream
- Chopped red onions
- Guacamole
- Cilantro
- Tortilla chips
- Salsa

Directions:

Step 1

Prepare the pasta according to the directions on the box.

Step 2

Preheat the oven's broiler.

Step 3

In a large oven-safe skillet, heat the oil over medium heat.

Step 4

Add the oil and corn and cook until the corn is defrosted. (Note: Continue cooking the corn for an additional 4 to 6 minutes, or until it begins to blacken in spots.)

Step 5

Combine the chicken, cumin, garlic, and paprika in a medium bowl. Sauté for 2 to 3 minutes, or until fragrant.

Step 6

Add the enchilada sauce, green chilies, and diced tomatoes and stir to combine.

Step 7

Cook for 2 to 3 minutes, or until the sauce begins to bubble.

Step 8

Turn off heat and add 1 cup of cheese, chicken, and pasta.

Step 9

Scatter the remaining cheese over the pasta. Broil for 3 to 4 minutes, or until the cheese is bubbly and melted.

Step 10

Instantly serve pasta with any desired toppings.

Nutrition Facts:

Per Serving:
- ✓ Calories 582
- ✓ Protein 39 g
- ✓ Carbohydrates 57 g
- ✓ Fat 22 g
- ✓ Sodium 362 mg
- ✓ Cholesterol 100 mg
- ✓ Potassium 476 mg
- ✓ Calcium 362 mg
- ✓ Fiber 3 g

Simple Beef Ragu

Total Time: 35 minutes

Servings: 4

Difficulty level: low

Ingredients:

- One tablespoon cooking oil
- One and a half lbs. ground beef
- Half teaspoon salt
- One-Fourth teaspoon black pepper
- Four chopped garlic cloves
- One tablespoon dried basil
- Two teaspoon dried oregano
- Half cup water
- One 28 ounce can crushed tomatoes
- One teaspoon sugar

Directions:

Step 1

Over medium heat, heat oil in a big heavy-bottomed skillet. Add the salt, beef, and pepper to hot oil.

Step 2

Cook beef, breaking it up with a spatula, for 8 to 12 minutes, or until cooked through.

Step 3

In a pressure cooker, combine garlic, cooked beef, dried basil, water, dried oregano, and crushed tomatoes.

Step 4

Stir thoroughly.

Step 5

Set pressure cooker to "sealing" and cook on full for 6 minutes.

Step 6

Allow 10 minutes for the sauce to automatically release, and then manually remove any remaining pressure.

Step 7

Sugar should be incorporated into the prepared sauce. Season the sauce to taste with pepper and salt or a pinch of sugar, if desired, until it tastes good.

Nutrition Facts:

Per Serving:

- ✓ Calories 278
- ✓ Protein 37 g
- ✓ Carbohydrates 3 g
- ✓ Fiber 1 g
- ✓ Fat 12 g
- ✓ Sodium 406 mg
- ✓ Cholesterol 105 mg
- ✓ Potassium 639 mg
- ✓ Calcium 59 mg

Spicy Pasta with Chicken

Total Time:

Servings: 8

Difficulty level: low

Ingredients:

- Three tablespoons plus one teaspoon homemade spice blend (unsalted)
- One and a half lbs. boneless, skinless chicken breasts
- Sixteen oz. penne pasta
- Three tablespoons extra virgin olive oil
- One medium green bell pepper
- Half medium diced sweet onion
- One medium red bell pepper
- Three minced cloves of garlic
- One medium yellow bell pepper
- One-Fourth cup green onions thinly sliced
- One-Fourth cup no salt added chicken broth
- Half cup half and half
- Two tablespoons unsalted butter
- Half cup grated parmesan cheese

Directions:

Step 1

If preparing your own spice blend, combine all ingredients and set aside.

Step 2

Begin cooking the pasta until it is done. If the pasta is finished ahead of schedule, drain and combine with 1 teaspoon of oil to prevent clumping and sticking, then set aside.

Step 3

Season each side of the chicken with 2 teaspoons of seasoning.

Step 4

In a broad skillet, heat the oil over medium heat. When the oil is hot, add 1 tablespoon. Place the chicken in the hot oil and cook on both sides. Reduce to a medium-low heat and continue cooking the chicken until it reaches 165°F, around 8-10 minutes.

Step 5

When the chicken is fried, transfer to a work surface to cool.

Step 6

Reduce to a medium-low heat and add the remaining 2 tablespoons of oil, followed by the onions. Fry until they're golden brown and semi-soft, around 2 minutes. Frequently stir.

Step 7

Add the peppers to the pan and toss with the leftover teaspoon of seasoning. Cook, stirring occasionally, for 4 minutes.

Step 8

Cook for 30 seconds before adding the garlic.

Step 9

Combine the butter, broth, and half and half in a medium bowl. Stir well and cook, stirring constantly, for 1 minute, or until the butter is melted.

Step 10

Remove from flame and mix in the Parmesan cheese until fully melted.

Step 11

Whisk the sauce mixture and vegetable into the boiling water with the noodles.

Step 12

Cut the chicken breasts into one inch strips and split evenly into eight sections.

Step 13

Arrange 1 cup pasta mixture on a plate and cover with a piece of chicken.

Step 14

Decorate with thinly sliced green onions.

Nutrition Facts:

Per Serving:
- ✓ Calories 467
- ✓ Cholesterol 79 mg
- ✓ Fat 16 g
- ✓ Carbohydrates 48 g
- ✓ Protein 32 g
- ✓ Fiber 3 g
- ✓ Sodium 187 mg
- ✓ Phosphorus 322 mg
- ✓ Calcium 102 mg
- ✓ Potassium 448 mg

Skillet Chicken Pasta with Crispy Sage

Total Time: 40 minutes

Servings: 6

Difficulty level: low

Ingredients:

- One lb. whole grain pasta
- Four leaves fresh sage
- Three tablespoons cooking oil
- One cubed chicken breast
- Two cups chicken broth (low-sodium)
- Two chopped cloves shallots
- Two medium cubed sweet potatoes
- One-Fourth cup grated parmesan cheese
- One-Fourth cup heavy cream

Directions:

Step 1

Prepare the pasta according to the directions on the box.

Step 2

Alternate method for crispy sage: In a broad skillet over medium-high heat, heat one tablespoon oil. Cook, stirring occasionally, until the sage changes color from a light to a dark shade of green, around 2 minutes. Move sage to a paper-towel covered plate using a slotted spoon. Re-heat skillet.

Step 3

In a skillet, heat 1 tablespoon of oil. While the oil is heating, season the chicken with salt and pepper. Sauté the chicken in heated oil until cooked through, around 4 to 8 minutes. Remove chicken to a bowl and re-heat pan.

Step 4

Add 1 tablespoon oil to the skillet, followed by the shallots. Saute shallots for 1 to 2 minutes, or until tender. Bring chicken stock and sweet potatoes to a simmer in the pan. Put the lid or foil on, and cook for 7 to 8 minutes, or until the sweet potatoes are tender.

Step 5

Remove pan from heat when potatoes are tender and mix in cooked pasta and chicken. Include heavy cream (if desired) and mix to blend.

Step 6

Season pasta with the parmesan cheese, sage, and salt and pepper to taste. Serve right away.

Nutrition Facts:

Per Serving:
- Calories 503
- Protein 18 g
- Carbohydrates 76 g
- Fat 15 g
- Sodium 193 mg
- Cholesterol 41 mg
- Potassium 468mg

- ✓ Calcium 83 mg
- ✓ Fiber 8 g

Chapter 10: Sea food

Broccoli Fettuccine and Creamy Shrimp

Total Time: 15 minutes

Servings: 4

Difficulty level: low

Ingredients:

- Four oz. fettuccine
- Three-Fourth pound frozen medium shrimp
- One and three-fourth cup broccoli florets
- One garlic clove
- Half teaspoon garlic powder
- Ten oz. cream cheese
- One-Fourth cup lemon juice
- One-Fourth cup half and half creamer
- Three-Fourth teaspoon ground peppercorns

- One-Fourth cup red bell pepper

Directions:

Step 1

Cook the pasta as directed on the package, omitting the salt.

Step 2

Cook broccoli during the final three minutes of cooking time. Drain. Maintain a comfortable temperature.

Step 3

Cook and mix the shrimp and garlic over medium heat for 2–3 minutes, or until the shrimp are cooked through, in a non-stick skillet.

Step 4

Combine the garlic powder, cream cheese, ground peppercorns, lemon juice, and half-and-half in a medium mixing bowl for 2 minutes while cooking and stirring.

Step 5

Toss the shrimp mixture and pasta together. Sprinkle bell pepper on top.

Nutrition Facts:

Per Serving:
- ✓ Calories 468
- ✓ Carbohydrates 28 g
- ✓ Protein 27 g
- ✓ Fat 28 g
- ✓ Sodium 374 mg
- ✓ Cholesterol 213 mg
- ✓ Potassium 469 mg

- ✓ Calcium 157 mg
- ✓ Phosphorus 335 mg
- ✓ Fiber 2.6 g

Fish Tacos

Total Time: 40 minutes

Servings: 6

Difficulty level: low

Ingredients:

- One and a half cups cabbage
- Half bunch cilantro
- Half cup red onion
- One garlic clove
- One pound cod fillets
- Two limes
- Half teaspoon ground cumin
- One-Fourth teaspoon black pepper
- Half teaspoon chili powder
- Twelve corn tortillas
- One tablespoon olive oil
- One-Fourth cup sour cream
- Half cup mayonnaise
- Two tablespoons milk

Directions:

Step 1

Prepare the cabbage by shredding it and chopping the onion and cilantro. Place aside. Mince the garlic.

Step 2

Arrange the fish fillets in a tray and drizzle half a lime juice over them. Sprinkle the minced garlic, cumin, chilli powder, black pepper, and olive oil over the fillets. Put it in the fridge for half hour, turning fillets to cover with marinade.

Step 3

Combine the mayonnaise, sour cream, milk, and half a lime juice to make salsa blanca and cool in the refrigerator.

Step 4

Preheat oven to broil. Wrap foil around broiler plate. Broil fish for about 10 minutes, or until the flesh becomes opaque and white, and the fish flakes easily. Remove from oven, allowing it to cool slightly before flaking the fish into large chunks.

Step 5

In a pan, warm the corn tortillas one at a time until soft and wet. To keep them warm, cover them in a clean dish towel.

Step 6

To assemble tacos, put a piece of fish in the centre of each tortilla and cover with cabbage, salsa blanca, cilantro, red onion, and lime wedges. If needed, add hot sauce.

Nutrition Facts:

Per Serving:
- ✓ Calories 363
- ✓ Carbohydrates 30 g

- ✓ Protein 18 g
- ✓ Fat 19 g
- ✓ Sodium 194 mg
- ✓ Cholesterol 40 mg
- ✓ Potassium 507 mg
- ✓ Calcium 138 mg
- ✓ Phosphorus 327 mg
- ✓ Fiber 4.3 g

Zesty Orange Tilapia

Total Time: 30 minutes

Servings: 4

Difficulty level:

Ingredients:

- Sixteen oz. tilapia
- One teaspoon ground black pepper
- Four teaspoons orange juice
- One cup julienned carrots
- Half cup sliced green onions
- Three-Fourth cup julienned celery
- Two teaspoons orange zest

Directions:

Step 1

Heat oven to 450° F.

Step 2

Combine the carrots, celery, green onions, and orange zest in a small bowl.

Step 3

Divide the tilapia into four equal parts. Remove four big sheets of foil and coat with a non-stick spray.

Step 4

Arrange 14 vegetables slightly off center on each piece of foil and place the fish on top with 1 teaspoon orange juice atop each. Season with freshly ground black pepper to taste.

Step 5

Fold and crimp the foil to create an envelope or pouch, and arrange the sheet packets on a baking tray. Bake for approximately 12 minutes. When done, the fish will easily separate with a fork.

Step 6

Extract the pouches and immediately put them on the plates. Due to the steam, exercise caution when opening.

Nutrition Facts:

Per Serving:
- ✓ Calories 133
- ✓ Cholesterol 57 mg
- ✓ Fat 2 g
- ✓ Sodium 97 mg
- ✓ Protein 24 g
- ✓ Carbohydrates 6 g

- ✓ Phosphorus 214 mg
- ✓ Fiber 1.7 g
- ✓ Potassium 543 mg
- ✓ Calcium 42 mg

Classic Spicy Shrimp and Linguine

Total Time: 25 minutes

Servings: 4

Difficulty level: low

Ingredients:

- Eight oz. linguine, dry
- Four tablespoons olive oil
- Two dozen large shrimp
- Two teaspoons garlic
- One teaspoon paprika
- Half teaspoon black pepper
- Four cups broccoli florets
- Half teaspoon dried oregano
- One teaspoon dried basil
- Two tablespoons parmesan cheese
- Half teaspoon crushed red pepper flakes
- Four lemon wedges

Directions:

Step 1

Bring a big pot of water to a simmer in the stovetop. Linguine should be cooked according to the box instructions.

Step 2

Toss the shrimp in half the olive oil (2 tablespoons), with all the garlic, half the paprika, and half the black pepper.

Step 3

In a broad skillet, heat the oil over medium heat. Cook the shrimp for approximately 4 to 5 minutes, or until they are fully opaque.

Step 4

Combine broccoli and 1/4 cup water in a microwave-safe dish. Microwave for 5 minutes, covered.

Step 5

Once the pasta is cooked, drain and re-introduce it to the pot. Combine the remaining black pepper, olive oil, paprika, and all of the oregano and basil in a large mixing bowl. Finally, stir in the parmesan cheese.

Step 6

When the shrimp and broccoli are finished cooking, combine them together and coat both with the paprika and garlic mixture.

Step 7

Arrange spaghetti on a plate first, followed by shrimp and broccoli. Each plate should have a lemon wedge squeezed over it. Adjust the amount of red pepper to taste; the more you add, the tangier it will be!

Nutrition Facts:

Per Serving

- ✓ Calories 402
- ✓ Potassium 366mg
- ✓ Cholesterol 60mg
- ✓ Fat 16g
- ✓ Sodium 364mg
- ✓ Protein 17g
- ✓ Carbohydrate 47g
- ✓ Fiber 5g
- ✓ Calcium 111mg

Creamy Shrimp and Broccoli Fettuccine

Total Time: 10 minutes

Servings: 4

Difficulty level: low

Ingredients:

- Four oz. fettuccine
- Three-Fourth pound frozen medium shrimp
- One and a half cup broccoli florets
- One garlic clove
- Half teaspoon garlic powder
- Ten oz. cream cheese
- One-Fourth cup lemon juice

- One-Fourth cup half and half creamer
- Three-Fourth teaspoon ground peppercorns
- One-Fourth cup red bell pepper

Directions:

Step 1

Cook the pasta as directed on the package, omitting the salt.

Step 2

Cook the broccoli during the final three minutes of cooking time. Drain. Maintain a comfortable temperature.

Step 3

Cook and mix the shrimp and garlic over medium heat for 2–3 minutes, or until the shrimp are cooked through, in a non-stick skillet.

Step 4

Combine the cream cheese, lemon juice, garlic powder, ground peppercorns, and half-and-half in a medium mixing bowl for 2 minutes cooking and stirring.

Step 5

Toss the shrimp and pasta mixture together. Sprinkle bell pepper on top.

Nutrition Facts:

Per Serving:
- ✓ Calories 468
- ✓ Carbohydrates 28 g
- ✓ Protein 27 g
- ✓ Fat 28 g
- ✓ Sodium 374 mg

- ✓ Cholesterol 213 mg
- ✓ Potassium 469 mg
- ✓ Calcium 157 mg
- ✓ Phosphorus 335 mg
- ✓ Fiber 2.6 g

Shrimp Fried Rice

Total Time: 10 minutes

Servings: 4

Difficulty level: low

Ingredients:

- Three by four cup onion
- One tablespoon fresh ginger root
- One garlic clove
- Three tablespoons scallions
- Three by four teaspoon black pepper
- Five tablespoons peanut oil
- One-Fourth teaspoon salt
- Half cup small pre-cooked shrimp
- Four beaten eggs
- One cup frozen peas and carrots
- Four cups white long-grain rice, cooked and cooled

Directions:

Step 1

Dice the onion and finely slice the scallions. Garlic and ginger root, minced.

Step 2

In a large non-stick skillet, heat 1 tablespoon oil over medium-high heat.

Step 3

Add half a teaspoon of black pepper and onion, and cook for around 2 minutes, or until onion is tender.

Step 4

Whisk in the garlic, ginger, and scallions for approximately 1 minute.

Step 5

Add shrimp and cook, stirring constantly, until heated through.

Step 6

Whisk in the peas and carrots until heated through. In a big covered cup, combine the shrimp and vegetable mixture.

Step 7

Re-introduce the pan to the heat and apply the remaining 2 tablespoons oil. Scramble the eggs in the skillet until they are cooked. Transfer eggs to a bowl along with the shrimp and vegetables.

Step 8

Reheat the pan and add 1 tablespoon of oil. Stir in four cups of cooked rice to rehydrate and spray with oil.

Step 9

Sprinkle the rice with pepper and salt and allow it to sit in skillet for approximately 2 minutes without stirring.

Step 10

Combine the rice, shrimp, vegetables, and eggs in a mixing bowl. Serve immediately.

Nutrition Facts:

Per Serving:

- ✓ Calories 421
- ✓ Carbohydrates 53 g
- ✓ Protein 16 g
- ✓ Fat 16 g
- ✓ Sodium 271 mg
- ✓ Cholesterol 244 mg
- ✓ Potassium 285 mg
- ✓ Calcium 71 mg
- ✓ Phosphorus 218 mg
- ✓ Fiber 2.5 g

Super Tuesday Shrimp

Total Time: 30 minutes

Servings: 4

Difficulty level: low

Ingredients:

- Four oz. pasta
- Two garlic cloves
- Two tablespoons onion
- One-Fourth cup feta cheese
- One tablespoon olive oil
- Twelve oz. medium shrimp

- One-Fourth cup sun dried tomatoes in oil
- Eight oz. frozen pea pods

Directions:

Step 1

Cook the pasta as directed on the box, omitting the salt. Drain and reserve.

Step 2

Finely mince the onion and garlic. Shrimp should be shelled and de-veined.

Step 3

Heat oil in a sauté pan and sauté garlic and onion until lightly browned.

Step 4

Combine the sun-dried tomatoes, shrimp, and pea pods in a medium bowl.

Step 5

Continue cooking until the shrimp changes color.

Step 6

Combine the shrimp and pasta.

Step 7

Garnish with feta cheese and serve.

Nutrition Facts:

Per Serving:
- ✓ Calories 302
- ✓ Carbohydrates 27 g
- ✓ Protein 26 g
- ✓ Fat 10 g
- ✓ Sodium 307 mg

- ✓ Cholesterol 142 mg
- ✓ Potassium 441 mg
- ✓ Calcium 160 mg
- ✓ Phosphorus 309 mg
- ✓ Fiber 3.5 g

Shrimp-Stuffed Deviled Eggs

Total Time: 20 minutes

Servings: 6

Difficulty level: low

Ingredients:

- Six large eggs, hard boiled
- Half teaspoon mustard
- Half cup cooked shrimp
- One and a half tablespoons mayonnaise
- One-Fourth teaspoon black pepper
- Half teaspoon lemon juice

Directions:

Step 1

Half cooked eggs lengthwise. Remove yolks carefully and put in a tub.

Step 2

Finely chop the shrimp and add to egg yolks along with mustard, mayonnaise, lemon juice, and pepper. Combine ingredients until well blended.

Step 3

Fill half of the egg whites with the yolk mixture and shrimp.

Nutrition Facts:

Per Serving:

- ✓ Calories 112
- ✓ Carbohydrates 1 g
- ✓ Protein 9 g
- ✓ Fat 8 g
- ✓ Sodium 113 mg
- ✓ Cholesterol 231 mg
- ✓ Potassium 93 mg
- ✓ Calcium 33 mg
- ✓ Phosphorus 122 mg
- ✓ Fiber 0 g

Honey Glazed Salmon

Total Time: 35 minutes

Servings: 4

Difficulty level: low

Ingredients:

- One pound salmon fillet skinned, deboned
- One tablespoon sesame oil (optional)
- Garlic Ginger Glaze
- Half inch cube ginger grated
- Three tablespoons honey
- Four tablespoons rice vinegar
- Four tablespoons soy sauce

- Three-Fourth garlic cloves, pressed

Directions:

Step 1

Mix 1 tablespoon of sesame oil, 3-4 pressed garlic cloves, 4 tablespoons of soy sauce, 3 tablespoons of sugar, 4 tablespoons of rice vinegar, and 1/2-inch grated ginger in a small saucepan. Cook, stirring occasionally, until thickened and reduced, around 10 minutes.

Step 2

Meanwhile, season both sides of the salmon fillet with crushed black pepper. Heat a couple of tablespoons oil in a skillet over high heat. Include the salmon, and fry until nicely golden on both sides, around 5-6 minutes per side, covered with a lid in between. This can take more or less time depending on the size of your salmon. Look for a salmon centre temperature of 145°F.

Step 3

Arrange the salmon fillets on a serving platter and drizzle with the honey glaze. Consume immediately.

Step 4

As a side dish, serve with rice. Broccoli, green beans, and asparagus also all make lovely additions to this meal.

Nutrition Facts:

Per Serving:
- ✓ Calories 258
- ✓ Cholesterol 62mg
- ✓ Fat 11g
- ✓ Sodium 1057mg
- ✓ Carbohydrates 15g

- ✓ Potassium 603mg
- ✓ Fiber 1g
- ✓ Calcium 21mg
- ✓ Protein 25g

Foil Baked Pimento Cod Fillet

Total Time: 10 minutes

Servings: 4

Difficulty level: low

Ingredients:

- Twelve oz. cod fillets
- One tablespoon olive oil
- One lemon
- Half teaspoon black pepper
- One-Fourth teaspoon salt
- Four oz. jar diced pimento peppers

Directions:

Step 1

Heat oven to 350° F.

Step 2

On the preparation board, lay out two big sheets of heavy-duty aluminium foil.

Step 3

Slice lemons rather thinly. Every piece of foil should have half a lemon slice.

Step 4

Arrange cod fillets in a single layer on the lemon slices, 2 fillets per foil.

Step 5

Season each fillet lightly with salt and pepper to taste.

Step 6

Drizzle each fillet with olive oil and sprinkle with diced pimentos.

Step 7

Fold the foil sides together to enclose the fish. Bake for 20 minutes on a baking sheet. To eat, remove the fillets from the foil.

Nutrition Facts:

Per Serving:
- ✓ Calories 112
- ✓ Carbohydrates 5 g
- ✓ Protein 16 g
- ✓ Fat 4 g
- ✓ Sodium 184 mg
- ✓ Cholesterol 37 mg
- ✓ Potassium 438 mg
- ✓ Calcium 33 mg
- ✓ Phosphorus 182 mg
- ✓ Fiber 1.8 g

Mediterranean Baked Trout

Total Time: 30 minutes

Servings: 3

Difficulty level: low

Ingredients:

- Half large fennel bulb, cored and thinly sliced
- Two tablespoons extra virgin olive oil
- Half large thinly sliced onion
- Four teaspoons spiced sea salt
- One-Fourth cup panko breadcrumbs
- Two rainbow trout butterflied fillets
- Six oz. cherry tomatoes, halved
- One lemon
- One-Fourth cup sliced pitted kalamata olives

Directions:

Step 1

Heat oven to 400° F and centre a baking rack in the oven. Arrange aluminum foil on a baking sheet and brush with olive oil cooking spray.

Step 2

Coat the sliced fennel and onion in 1 teaspoon Mediterranean Spiced Sea Salt. Distribute evenly on the lined baking sheet. Bake for 10 minutes, or until the fennel softens and starts to caramelize.

Step 3

Take the baking sheet out of the oven and place the trout fillets on it. Distribute panko breadcrumbs and remaining 3 teaspoons of sea salt equally. Over the fish, scatter sliced olives, halved tomatoes, and lemon slices.

Step 4

Switch to oven and bake for an additional 5 minutes, then broil for an additional 3–5 minutes, or until the breadcrumbs are nicely browned and the fish is baked through. Keep an eye

on it to prevent the breadcrumbs from burning. Remove from oven and halve the fillets. Distribute vegetables evenly among serving plates and serve with fish. Enjoy!

Nutrition Facts:

Per Serving:
- ✓ Calories 110
- ✓ Carbohydrates 6 g
- ✓ Protein 15 g
- ✓ Fat 3 g
- ✓ Sodium 180 mg
- ✓ Cholesterol 35 mg
- ✓ Potassium 420 mg
- ✓ Calcium 30 mg
- ✓ Phosphorus 170 mg
- ✓ Fiber 1.5 g

Shrimp Scampi

Total Time: 10 minutes

Servings: 4

Difficulty level:

Ingredients:

- One-Fourth cup all-purpose flour
- One teaspoon crushed red pepper
- Half teaspoon ground black pepper
- One pound shrimp
- Two minced garlic cloves
- Four tablespoons canola oil
- Two tablespoons white wine
- Two tablespoons (cubed) butter
- One-Fourth cup lemon juice
- One tablespoon chopped parsley

Directions:

Step 1

Mix the black pepper, flour, and red pepper flakes in a big mixing bowl.

Step 2

Coat the shrimp uniformly with the flour mixture.

Step 3

Heat 1/2 of the canola oil in a large nonstick skillet over medium-high heat.

Step 4

Cook for 2 to 3 minutes on either side, or until the shrimp are cooked through.

Hence, in this cookbook, you will find all the recipes according to your needs and wants. Because of this book, you can enjoy everything you like without worrying; you just have to watch your portion size according to your weight and age.

With time as CKD (chronic kidney disease) worsens, dietary needs increase. A health care provider is recommended who can guide a patient regarding his/her food choices.

Conclusion

Consumption of food and beverages has an impact on one's health. Living a healthy lifestyle and following a balanced, low-salt, low-fat diet will help you manage your blood pressure. If you have diabetes, you can effectively regulate your blood sugar by making prudent food and beverage choices. Managing diabetes and high bp can aid in preventing the progression of kidney disease.

A kidney-friendly diet can also help prevent further damage to your kidneys. A kidney-friendly diet restricts specific foods to avoid mineral accumulation in the body.

For all diet plans, including the renal diet, you must keep track of your intake of specific nutrients, such as:

- Calories
- Fats
- Carbohydrates
- Proteins

To ensure that you are receiving the recommended quantities of these components, you must eat and drink in the recommended portions. The "Nutrition Facts" labeling that appears alongside the rrecipes in this cookbook contains all of the details you need to keep a record of your intake.

Your food and drink choices while on hemodialysis may have a significant impact on how you feel and how well your treatments perform.

Between dialysis sessions, wastes will accumulate in your blood and cause illness. You can minimize waste accumulation by exercising self-control over what you consume.

Everyone's calorie requirements are unique. If you are overweight, you may need to reduce your caloric intake, or you may need to find ways to increase your caloric intake if you are dropping weight without trying.

Nutrition Facts:

Per Serving:

- ✓ Calories 295
- ✓ Carbohydrates 17g
- ✓ Protein 40g
- ✓ Fat 9g
- ✓ Potassium: 166
- ✓ Fiber 7g
- ✓ Sodium: 196
- ✓ Phosphorus: 220
- ✓ Cholesterol 35 mg
- ✓ Calcium 30 mg

- One-Fourth teaspoon black pepper
- Two halved lemons
- Two tablespoons finely chopped fresh herbs

Directions:

Step 1

In a big saucepan, place a steamer. Add water until it reaches just below it.

Step 2

Increase the heat to high and bring to a simmer. Include the vegetables and cover with a lid.

Step 3

Steam for approximately 7 minutes, or until tender.

Step 4

Sprinkle with 1/4 teaspoon of the salt and transfer to a cup. Cover to maintain a comfortable temperature.

Step 5

Add additional water to the pan if necessary. Bring down to a boil. Season with the leftover salt and pepper to taste.

Step 6

Place the halibut in the steamer, cover with a lid and cook for around 7 minutes, or until it is uniform in colour throughout.

Step 7

Drizzle the oil over the halibut and vegetables. Sprinkle with herbs and serve alongside the lemon halves.

Nutrition Facts:

Per Serving:
- ✓ Calories 664
- ✓ Fiber 14
- ✓ Fat 26g
- ✓ Protein 42g
- ✓ Sodium 0.3g
- ✓ Cholesterol 70 mg
- ✓ Carbohydrates 13 g
- ✓ Phosphorus 138 mg
- ✓ Calcium 13 mg
- ✓ Potassium 223 g

Steamed Fish and Vegetables

Total Time: 25 minutes

Servings: 4

Difficulty level: low

Ingredients:

- One head broccoli florets
- Three-Fourth teaspoon kosher salt
- Three zucchini
- Four 8 oz. skinless 1 inch thick halibut fillets
- Four teaspoons extra-virgin olive oil

- Two 400g cans chopped tomatoes
- 400ml vegetable bouillon made with two teaspoons vegetable bouillon powder
- Two green peppers
- One lime zest
- 160 grams brown basmati rice
- 400 grams can and 210 grams can red kidney beans
- Some fresh chopped coriander
- Some chopped leaf parsley
- 550 grams pack frozen wild salmon, skinned and cut into large pieces

Directions:

Step 1

In a large non-stick skillet, heat the oil and roast the onions for 10 minutes, or until softened and golden. Combine the garlic, spring onions, chilli, and thyme in a medium bowl. Cook, stirring constantly, for 1 minute. Incorporate the bouillon and tomatoes, followed by the peppers. Cover and boil for 15 minutes.

Step 2

In the meantime, prepare the rice as per the package directions. Stir in the coriander, beans, and parsley, and continue cooking gently for an additional 10 minutes, or until the peppers are ready. Cook for 4-5 minutes, or until the salmon is cooked through.

Step 3

Distribute half of the stew between two bowls and garnish with coriander sprigs. Cool the remainder of the stew, then cover and chill until a later date. Re-heat gently in a saucepan until bubbly.

Arrange brown rice and broccoli on the side. Keep leftovers refrigerated for up to three days.

Nutrition Facts:

Per Serving:

- ✓ Calories 187.29
- ✓ Protein 22.17 g
- ✓ Fat 10.46 g
- ✓ Fiber 0.00 g
- ✓ Cholesterol 165 mg
- ✓ Sodium 41.53 mg
- ✓ Carbohydrates 20 g
- ✓ Calcium 0 mg
- ✓ Potassium 349.7 mg

Spicy fish stew

Total Time: 40 minutes

Servings: 4

Difficulty level: low

Ingredients:

- One tablespoon olive oil
- Two thinly sliced onions
- Three chopped spring onions
- Three chopped garlic cloves
- One thinly sliced red chili
- A few thyme sprigs

- ✓ Potassium 349.7 mg
- ✓ Protein 17.5 g
- ✓ Fiber 6 g
- ✓ Calcium 0 mg

Seared Tuna Steak

Total Time: 5 minutes

Servings: 5

Difficulty level: low

Ingredients:

- Two tablespoons butter, unsalted
- Pinch of grounded black pepper
- One pound tuna
- Whole black pepper
- Three tablespoons olive oil
- Two tablespoons taste Of Louisiana

Directions:

Step 1

Melt the butter in a saucepan and brush tuna with it.

Step 2

Add Taste of Louisiana seasoning and pepper to taste.

Step 3

Heat olive oil in a medium saucepan over medium-high heat. Sear the tuna for 2 minutes on either side.

Step 4

Step 2

In a wok or large skillet, heat 1 teaspoon coconut oil over medium-high heat.

Step 3

Prepare a plate by lining it with paper towels.

Step 4

Add the shrimp to the wok and cook for approximately 2 minutes, stirring continuously. Remove to the prepared plate until they are pink and scarcely opaque.

Step 5

Add the red bell pepper, cabbage, and scallion whites to the wok along with the remaining one teaspoon coconut oil. Stir-fry for approximately 3 minutes, or until the cabbage is crisp-tender.

Step 6

Stir the mixture of cornstarch into the shrimp and add it to the wok.

Step 7

Cook, stirring continuously, for approximately 2 minutes, or until the sauce has thickened and the shrimp is coated.

Step 8

Remove from heat and garnish with scallion greens.

Nutrition Facts:

Per Serving:
- ✓ Calories 209
- ✓ Cholesterol 165 mg
- ✓ Fat 5.6 g
- ✓ Sodium 963.8 mg
- ✓ Carbohydrates 20 g

- ✓ Sodium 50 mg
- ✓ Phosphorus 138 mg
- ✓ Calcium 13 mg
- ✓ Potassium 223 g

Shrimp and Cabbage Stir-Fry

Total Time: 15 minutes

Servings: 2

Difficulty level: low

Ingredients:

- One tablespoon cornstarch
- Two scallions
- Half cup cold water
- One teaspoon sriracha or other hot sauce
- One tablespoon low-sodium tamari or soy sauce
- One tablespoon minced fresh ginger
- Two teaspoons coconut oil
- Two minced garlic cloves
- One-Third head green cabbage
- Half pound large shrimp
- One medium red bell pepper

Directions:

Step 1

Mix the water, cornstarch, soy sauce or tamari, and sriracha in a small cup. Combine the garlic and ginger in a large mixing bowl until well combined, then set aside.

Directions:

Step 1

Heat oven to 425° F. Oil a 913 glass baking bowl.

Step 2

Using a paper towel, pat fish dry on both sides, then cut fillets in half lengthwise.

Step 3

Whisk together the egg, paprika, water, and garlic powder in a shallow bowl. In a separate dish, combine seasoning blend and cornmeal.

Step 4

Working with 1 piece of fish at a time, dip it into the egg mixture and then gently cover it with the cornmeal mixture. In a baking dish, place the coated fish. Repeat with each fish piece.

Step 5

Bake for 15 minutes, or until the fish is cooked through and lightly browned. During the cooking process, turn once.

Step 6

Serve immediately with a squeeze of fresh lemon.

Nutrition Facts:

Per Serving:
- ✓ Calories 170
- ✓ Cholesterol 70 mg
- ✓ Fat 5 g
- ✓ Carbohydrates 13 g
- ✓ Protein 16 g
- ✓ Fiber 1 g

> ✓ Fiber 1.5 g

Oven Fried Fish

Total Time: 20 minutes

Servings: 8

Difficulty level: low

Ingredients:

- Three tablespoons canola oil
- Two beaten eggs
- One and a half pound of white fish fillets
- One tablespoon of water
- Half teaspoon garlic powder
- One teaspoon paprika
- One cup cornmeal
- One tablespoon salt-free seasoning blend
- Lemon wedges

Homemade seasoning blends:

- Half teaspoon garlic powder
- Half teaspoon black pepper
- Half teaspoon onion powder
- Half teaspoon cayenne pepper
- Half teaspoon dried thyme
- Half teaspoon dried oregano

Step 5

Transfer prepared shrimp to a tray or baking sheet to cool.

Step 6

Mix the garlic, chicken broth or wine, and lemon juice in the same pan.

Step 7

Stir the mixture with a wooden spoon and heat until it comes to a boil.

Step 8

Remove from heat and gradually mix in the cold butter until it is fully incorporated.

Step 9

Re-introduce the shrimp to the pan.

Step 10

Toss or stir in parsley until shrimp is coated. Serve.

Nutrition Facts:

Per Serving:

- ✓ Potassium: 166
- ✓ Sodium: 196
- ✓ Phosphorus: 220
- ✓ Calories 110
- ✓ Carbohydrates 6 g
- ✓ Protein 15 g
- ✓ Fat 3 g
- ✓ Cholesterol 35 mg
- ✓ Calcium 30 mg